Praise for Dog Church . . .

"Touching the cord that runs between events that shape us and our relationships with dogs and infused with a sense of marvel at the true and boundless love that they bestow upon us, *Dog Church* explores the profound sense of loss with which we must contend when a beloved dog passes and the solace to be found in the joy of recalling a relationship which has made us the better for it."—Larry Levin, *New York Times* bestselling author of *Oogy: The Dog Only a Family Could Love*

"Written with astounding grace and tenderness, Gail Gilmore's *Dog Church* is a powerful meditation on what it means to be saved by a dog, and what it takes to return that gift in the most trying times. A beautiful testament to the sacred, healing, and transformative bond between human and canine, *Dog Church* invites us to find peace in heartbreak and faith in the hereafter, and to look within at our own endless capacity for devotion and for love."—Rita Zoey Chin, author, *Let the Tornado Come*

DOG

CHURCH

GAIL GILMORE

DOG
CHURCH

GusGus Press • Bedazzled Ink Publishing
Fairfield, California

978-1-945805-06-6 paperback
978-1-945805-07-3 epub
978-1-945805-08-0 mobi

Cover artwork
Stephen Huneck

Cover Photo
Amanda McDermott

Cover Design
by

DESIGNS

GusGus Press
a division of
Bedazzled Ink Publishing Company
Fairfield, California
http://www.bedazzledink.com

For the tribe

ACKNOWLEDGMENTS

I am enormously and eternally grateful to the following people:

Mary Allen, Sorche Fairbank, and Kent Wolf, each of whom touched one version or another of this book in a significant way and provided it with new direction and life.

C.A. Casey at GusGus Press, who believed in the book and gave it a home.

Cher Tate, for providing her time, assistance, and legal expertise.

Nancy Love Robertson, Nore Rogers, and Bella Travaglini read early drafts and offered thoughtful suggestions along with endless amounts of encouragement.

Rita Zoey Chin and Larry Levin, who agreed to read a stranger's book and then wrote the kind of blurbs a first-time author dreams of.

Jon Ide graciously allowed me to use Stephen Huneck's artwork on the book's cover, and Amanda McDermott at the Stephen Huneck Gallery took the perfect photo.

Stephen Huneck, for the legacy of the Dog Chapel and Dog Mountain; Gwendolyn Ide Huneck, for refusing to let that legacy die; and the staff who carry it on in their absence.

Dr. Joy Lucas, for leaving her words behind in the Dog Chapel and for allowing me to share them. They changed everything.

Dr. Maija Curtis and Dr. Andrew Farabaugh, who provided Chispa with expert and compassionate care under difficult circumstances.

Dr. Bari Spielman, for caring for Chispa (and me) throughout Chispa's life, and most especially for being there at the last. "Thank you" will never be enough.

Dorothy Austin, for setting me on the path.

My mother Bibi M. Gilmore for passing down the gift, and my father C. Philip Gilmore for instilling in me an early love of the written word, and nurturing it with books brought home just because.

To the dogs and cats who've shared my life: You live in my heart, now and always.

And to Marisel Perez, who was there through it all: You are my heart.

"Love, light & peace to all who enter here. Thank you for this place sacred to dogs and we who love them."
—Dog Chapel, Vestibule

ONE

I BECOME A congregant of the Dog Chapel on the most ordinary of days. Driving west on Route 2, on the outskirts of St. Johnsbury, Vermont, I'm headed to my favorite Northeast Kingdom shoe store. It carries a surprising array of up-scale brands for these parts, and I love shopping there. No hassle, no pressure, just gorgeous shoes and the smell of brand new leather—the perfect place in which to spend a mindless hour or two on a Saturday afternoon.

Up ahead on the right, just beyond the big red Farmer's Daughter Gift Barn, I see the sign for the Dog Chapel. This is not the first time I've driven this stretch of Route 2, not the first time I've noticed the unusual sign with the life-size dog walker and pack of leashed dogs poised atop a tall granite base, an arrow beneath the words "Dog Chapel" pointing the way up a dirt road. I've always been curious about the Dog Chapel, but for whatever reason have never taken the time to visit. Next time, I invariably tell myself. Definitely next time.

And now, on this Saturday afternoon, I find myself inexplicably drawn to the sign, curious about what lies in the direction of the pointing arrow. What is this place? Could it actually be a chapel for dogs? Unlikely, I think, but if it is, who created it—and why? The sudden need to know the answers to these questions is absolute and overwhelming, and I pull off the main road to investigate.

I drive slowly up the longer and bumpier than expected dirt road, pull into a small unpaved parking lot, and get out of the car. Walking across the expansive lawn toward the chapel, I pass a small pond and a Colonial-style white building with a sign that reads "Gallery." This, I soon learn, is the gallery of artist and author Stephen Huneck, who considers the Dog Chapel, meant to celebrate the unbreakable bonds between dogs and the people who love them, his most significant piece of work.

I don't know what I'd expected, but when the Dog Chapel comes into view I'm astonished by what I see. The chapel, about the size of a one-room-schoolhouse, looks exactly like a nineteenth-century New England village church, right down to its white clapboards and high steeple. But when I take a closer look at the steeple, it's clear that the similarity to a traditional village church ends there. On top of this steeple, where I expect to see a cross, there's instead a carving—a gilded, winged Labrador retriever poised as if in flight toward heaven.

The doors to the Dog Chapel are open, the invitation obvious. As I approach the entrance, the sign near the steps makes me smile: "Welcome. All creeds, all breeds, no dogmas allowed." Good words to live by. For a moment, I envision what the world might look like if this sign, its words translated into thousands of languages, were posted outside every place of worship, all across the planet.

A recording of what sounds like Native American flute music, audible from outside the chapel, redirects my focus from visions of religious peace, harmony, and pluralism back to the present. The notes of the music are ethereal and haunting, and I follow them into the chapel.

Inside, I immediately notice a stack of brochures and a pile of colored index cards placed neatly on a long wooden table in the chapel's vestibule. I open a brochure and glance through it quickly. It recounts the history of the Dog Chapel, along with why it came into being, and provides a brief bio of Stephen Huneck. I slip one into my shoulder bag.

As I turn my full attention to the space around me, I realize that the walls are covered with randomly placed drawings, photographs, index cards, and post-its, creating a collage of vivid and overlapping color. When I approach the wall for a closer look, what I see amazes me. On every one of those index cards and post-its is a hand-written message for a deceased pet, left by a visitor to the chapel.

"To my loving dog Bear: I loved you more than anything in the world and no dog will ever replace you in my heart . . . Thanks for being there when no one else was."

"My loves Butter & Bonnye—My best friends who changed my life and saw me through so many changes. I miss you over and over again, seeing you in so many other blessed dogs."

"You were my best friend. I'll love you forever. I miss you every day. Still. I wish I could have allowed you to live forever."

"Hannah: Tevy—My girls—I miss you so. Wait for me."

"Riley—Run free, my wonderful friend. We love you always."

"For my sweet little Ruby, who was my solace & my comfort through the dark nights of my childhood."

These messages resonate deeply with me. Even more curious now to see the rest of the Dog Chapel, I walk into the sanctuary. Inside the small, softly-lit space are five hand-carved and polished pews. The pews show touches of the artist's whimsy, their benches supported on each side by carved, painted dogs sitting in profile—four black Labs, four golden retrievers, and two yellow Labs. Placed throughout the sanctuary are life-size, true-to-breed dogs that Huneck has carved from wood, and the chapel's windows are stained glass scenes depicting not the lives of saints and martyrs, but the life of a black Lab. At the bottom of each window is a word, the Word of Dog: Peace, Play, Joy, Friend, Trust, Faith, and Love.

On the floor near the front of the chapel, where an altar would normally stand, a well-worn hooked rug depicts two Labs engaged in a game of tug-o-war. The caption beneath the design reads "Love is Give and Take."

Holy smokes, I say to myself. It's like dog church in here.

I've never seen anything like it.

I sit in the rear pew and take in the details of my surroundings, and it's at this moment that the full impact of the Dog Chapel hits me. Just as in the vestibule, nearly every square inch of the sanctuary's walls, from floor to ceiling, is covered with index cards, post-its, drawings, and photographs. The entire Dog Chapel is a Wall of Remembrance—one great big love letter to dogs loved and lost but never forgotten.

This place is more than dog church—it's Dog Church.

As I sit in the sanctuary of the Dog Chapel, surrounded by the loving memories of people whose animals have changed their lives, I take a few moments to remember my own animals. I picture their shapes and colors, their individual markings and characteristics—the white blaze on a neck and chest, the tufted feet, the black spots on a nose, the long pointed ears that, depending on mood, stood straight up, folded themselves backward along a slender head, or stuck out sideways, like ears made of origami paper. I speak their names into the emptiness of the chapel: Nike, Lucy, Pez, Comet. What gifts their lives were to me, and how deeply I still miss their presence.

But I think, too, of my living animals—Laika, Chispa, Martina, and Mandu—and the ways in which they reflect God's unconditional love back to me in every moment of their existence. Alone in the Dog Chapel's sanctuary, the flute music a backdrop to my memories, I realize with some surprise that I've never felt closer to God than in this tiny church filled with testaments of love, loss, and grief. I begin to feel as if something truly extraordinary might happen to me here.

WHEN MY FOURTEEN-year-old black Lab Nike died, I called in sick for several days. She was the first of my dogs to die, and I was completely unprepared for the deep and raw grief I experienced—a grief so incapacitating that even the simplest tasks of daily living seemed, for the first few days, overwhelming and impossible. On the day I returned to work, I decided not to tell my colleagues why I'd been out. I was terrified of hearing, either outright or implied, the words "She was just a dog." The idea that my colleagues might even think those words, regardless of whether or not they spoke them, was enough to make me choose not to share with them what had been a very significant life event for me.

Nike's death taught me that grief can be one of life's most isolating experiences, particularly when one grieves the loss of a pet. But sitting in the Dog Chapel now, surrounded by the remembrances of others who grieve their deceased pets as deeply as I grieve my own, provides a sense of connection to a vast though unknown community of people like me—people who love their animals with their whole heart, who understand the ways in which the wordless and unconditional love of an animal can change everything. "Just a dog" doesn't exist in our communal lexicon. Instead, the words left behind by visitors to the Dog Chapel are like a silent conversation in which thousands of dog-bereft people reach out to one another and say, "Yes. I understand."

It's this feeling of connectedness to those who've visited the Dog Chapel before me that inspires me to get up from the pew and walk over to the back wall of the chapel. I want to bear witness to the love and grief of those who've written the thousands of notes stuck to the chapel walls, and to the joyful lives of the animals who have inspired those words. I look at a few more photographs, read a few more cards. Almost immediately, I wish I hadn't.

Drawn to a particular photograph, I don't realize until I begin to read the words beneath it that this remembrance is for

a shelter dog. He is beautiful—white with golden brown spots
on his haunches, ears and patches on either side of his face the
same shade of golden brown as his spots, and a white muzzle.
His tail is up, his head slightly down, as he looks at the person
taking the photograph. He stands in a shelter pen, water and
food bowls nearby. I love this dog at first sight.

The remembrance, written by a shelter worker, doesn't fit
on an index card; it's written on a large sheet of white paper.
I can't bear to read it in its entirety. The woman who writes
about this dog describes her grief at having to put down dogs
no one remembers or cares about. As I stand in the chapel's
sanctuary, where the animals remembered are people's
cherished pets, I'm grateful to this woman for bringing to
mind all the others. No individual tributes will be written and
left on the walls of the Dog Chapel for these abandoned dogs,
but she speaks for them, remembers them, in a way that spares
the reader no detail and no pain.

I'm completely unraveled by what I read, but the one small
part of that emotionally naked remembrance I choose to take
with me is this: "On this day in May there were enough tears
to make the brightest, biggest rainbow especially for you, as
you passed over the bridge and met your old and new friends
waiting . . . Please say we will meet again, for the first time,
someday . . . I hope every day there is a sunny day in May so
you can romp and play . . . never look back here where humans
hurt and failed you . . . I will never forget you." I hold onto
those words tightly.

Gradually I become aware of the presence of another
woman in the Dog Chapel, and make an effort to contain the
intense emotions that have now rushed to the surface. But
despite my attempts, the tears rise up and over the rims of my
eyes in one quick and fluid motion—tears for the shelter dogs,
for the loss of my own animals, and for the collective loss
represented by every one of the photographs and notes pinned
to the chapel walls.

Eventually my emotions drown themselves, and I walk
slowly into the vestibule, pick up a small pastel-orange index

card, and write a little love letter of my own. I then walk back into the sanctuary, climb up a small step ladder, and attach the card to the rear sanctuary wall with a pushpin, careful not to obscure other people's memories with my own. I climb back down the ladder and sit for a few moments on the bottom step, exhausted by all that's transpired in this place. And then, what I consider to be a little miracle happens.

Across from the step ladder a gangly, long-haired black dog lies on the floor, observing me quietly. I assume the dog belongs to the woman I noticed earlier in the vestibule. Glancing over at the dog, I feel there's something about her, something in the positioning of her body on the floor and the way she looks up at me, that's so familiar. I watch her for a few seconds more before making the connection—she reminds me of Nike. I extend my hand toward her slowly, tentatively.

The dog gets up from the floor and walks over to where I sit. She stands in front of me and gently licks my face, then my hands, in a purposeful way that seems to hold an intent known only to her. As the dog's tongue moves softly across my hand, I feel a rush of what I can only describe as the purest form of love sweep through my body. The sensation is fleeting, there and then gone, like a ghost.

But it happens.

It's as if I've been touched by something that's deeply known, yet beyond understanding. I wonder if perhaps in this place, for a very brief moment in time, one of my dogs has managed to reach through the liminal barrier between the living and the dead and, through this dog, touch and comfort me one more time. As I contemplate the possibility and meaning of this, the grief that overwhelmed me just moments earlier is transcended. I rub my hand along her neck, whispering over and over, "You're a special girl."

As the dog and I sit there together, the woman enters the sanctuary from the vestibule. She walks over to the wall and places her index card near the shelter dog's remembrance. She notices me watching her, and hesitates a moment before speaking.

"Did you happen to read the letter about the dog in the shelter?" she asks.

I nod. "That was a tough one . . . it pretty much undid me."

"I know what you mean. I volunteer at an animal shelter in the South. It's a kill shelter, so that letter brings up a lot of pain and anger for me. It's almost unbearable, reading it."

After a short silence, I ask what her dog's name is.

"Her name's Annie. She came from the shelter I volunteer at."

I tell her about the way Annie comforted me, and although I want to share my belief that the soul of one of my own dogs, dead now for nearly nine years, reached out to me through Annie, I stop just short of doing so. The feeling of resurrection that's come from my interaction with Annie feels too personal, too impossible to articulate. I've been touched by God in this place, and I know it. What I don't know is how to explain it.

Instead, the woman and I smile at each other and shake our heads slightly. We stand there together for a moment, eyes on Annie. I want to commit the dog to memory, every last detail of her. I watch her intently, taking in the color and texture of her fur, her wagging tail, her smile, the warmth and depth of her brown eyes and the love that radiates from them.

Out of nowhere, a silent prayer for her takes shape in my mind: May you live a long and happy life, may you be comforted as you have comforted others, and may the unconditional love you give with such joy come back to you over and over, now and forever. Amen.

I say goodbye to the woman, then run my hand over Annie's head one last time before leaving the chapel. I know I'll be back, but can't yet begin to imagine the way in which this tiny chapel overlooking Vermont farmland and built on a hill called Dog Mountain will become, over the years, one of the most sacred places in my spiritual landscape.

TWO

IT'S ABOUT TWENTY-FIVE minutes from St. Johnsbury to Littleton, New Hampshire, where my spouse Marisel and I have a vacation home, but I make the drive in a little less than twenty. My mind ignores the speed limit signs, instead pulling up image after unforgettable image of carved dogs and stained glass windows, notes and photographs, and Annie. I can't wait to share my discovery with Marisel. I pull the Jeep into the driveway, the tires crunching the loose gravel beneath them. That sound is the alert for our dogs, their cue to begin a frenzied yet oddly harmonic barking, meant as either welcome or warning depending on who you are and how you smell. I glance up at the living room window and spot them, Laika and Chispa, their heads just visible above the windowsill.

"Hey, girls," I call to them as I get out of the car.

At the sound of my voice, the barking morphs into excited whining and their heads disappear from view. They race over to the glass storm door to greet me as I walk up the steps onto the front porch.

Marisel isn't inside. I walk through the dining room, open the sliding glass door onto the back porch, and stand there for a moment gazing at the view of the mountains across the Connecticut River. I've stared at those mountains more times than I can remember, yet the sight of them never grows old for me. I loved them from the moment I saw them. They're beautiful, yes, but I love them for a different reason—for their constancy, their permanence. They will absolutely outlive me, those mountains, and loving them feels to me about as emotionally safe as love ever gets.

Looking out into the back yard I see Marisel in the vegetable garden, down near the edge of the woods. I walk back inside and grab the dogs' leashes from the shelf at the top of the basement stairs.

"C'mon, girls—let's go out!"

Hooking them up to their leashes, I stop for a moment to kiss their heads. They're so different, these two. Laika is shy around people and animals she doesn't know, Chispa fears no one. They're on opposite ends of the physical spectrum, too. Chispa's coat is very short, with coloring and markings that remind me of what a bonsai German Shepherd might look like if such a dog existed. Laika's coat is longer, a thick wavy blond with an undercoat perfectly suited for New England weather. They even smell different. Laika's head has a fresh, clean smell, like a lingering bath. But Chispa's head has a way of retaining the outdoors, and as I bend down to kiss her I inhale the comingled scent of sun and earth.

We walk together down to the garden, where Marisel is gathering the summer's last vegetables. As we get closer, I see that she's in the cucumber patch, sitting back on her heels, a gloved hand resting on her knee. Her head is bent forward as she pokes around the lower vines, looking for any cucumbers she might've missed.

She loves to garden, to dig her hands deep into the earth and make things grow. It's not a passion we share. The black flies, mosquitoes, and deer flies, along with the dirt that manages to work its way through garden gloves and become wedged under my fingernails, just aren't my idea of a good time. But gardening makes Marisel feel close to the earth, to the natural rhythm of the seasons. I'm glad we have enough acreage for a large garden.

She looks up to see me approaching with the dogs.

"Hey, Peapod. Did you find anything good at the store?"

She smiles as she drops a perfectly shaped cucumber into her vegetable bag.

I stare at her blankly for a few seconds until I remember that the reason for my going to St. Johnsbury had been to shop at my favorite shoe store.

"No, I never made it there. But I found something else that was absolutely amazing."

"What?"

"The Dog Chapel."

"The what?"

"The Dog Chapel. We've gone by the sign before, right past the Farmer's Daughter. Remember?"

"Oh, yeah—the place we always say we'll stop at next time."

"So I guess today was 'next time' for me, because I felt compelled to go see it. And guess what? It's a little church, for dogs and dog people. It's incredible. I've never seen anything like it in my life."

I describe the notes and pictures, the carved dogs, the pews, the stained glass windows, the ethereal Native American flute music.

"You have to see this place."

"I don't know . . . it sounds beautiful, but really sad. I don't think I could read all those notes on the walls. Too depressing."

"It's sad, but I don't think I'd call it depressing. It's actually really affirming to see that there are so many other people who love their animals the way we do."

Marisel is quiet for a few moments, and I know her well enough to know exactly what she's thinking: losing our animals has been so painful; what's to be gained by re-opening old wounds? But I also know the depth of her curiosity, and don't think she'll be able to resist seeing the Dog Chapel for herself.

"Okay, Pea. Let's go tomorrow morning before we head back home."

THE NEXT MORNING we have an early breakfast before driving over to the Dog Chapel. We discuss bringing the dogs with us, but in the end decide against it. For reasons I suspect have their origin in things that happened prior to our adopting them, Laika and Chispa aren't particularly comfortable or well-behaved around other dogs. I want Marisel to be able to enjoy her first visit to the Dog Chapel without worrying about our dogs making a scene there. Maybe next time, we agree.

As we drive up the dirt road leading to the Dog Chapel, I glance over at Marisel behind the wheel. She's unusually quiet, and I wonder if she's sorry she agreed to come. Her expression, eyes fixed straight ahead, gives away nothing. As we approach the end of the road she finally speaks.

"Where do I go, straight or right?"

"Take a right, and park in the lot at the end."

We park the Jeep and get out, then walk past the gallery and across the lawn to the Dog Chapel. I experience a strong sense of déjà-vu—sun shining, chapel doors open, flute music ethereal and beckoning. Marisel stops for a moment to admire a cluster of life-size, painted carvings standing just outside the chapel—a man in a suit surrounded by a pack of dogs of all sizes and breeds.

"It's amazing. They all look so real."

"I know, it's really incredible, but wait'll you see the inside of the chapel."

I take her hand and we walk in together. She looks at the walls of the vestibule, covered with notes and photographs, but doesn't stop to read any of them. That, I know, will come later. We walk into the sanctuary, and she's as captivated as I'd been the first time I saw it.

"Look at these pews—my God, how beautiful. Look at the details, the way the dog's fur curls, the way the tail's feathered. And the seats are almost like mirrors . . . it must've taken such a long time to get all the wood to shine like that."

I smile at her delight, realize how much I'd wanted her to love the Dog Chapel. I point out the stained glass windows to her.

"Wow. Those are gorgeous. I can't believe one person built this whole chapel. It must've taken forever. And to be so talented with both wood and glass . . . it's amazing."

She's right. It's absolutely amazing.

We settle in one of the pews, taking it all in. The music lends an aura of sacredness to the space, and we sit together in contemplative silence. After a while I ask if she wants to read some of the notes. She agrees, and we get up and walk to the back of the chapel. As we make our way along the wall, we begin reading some of the notes to each other.

> "Autumn—You were taken from us too soon.
> Though your life was short lived with us, we can
> still feel your presence. You brought us love, laughter,
> and joy. We all miss you. Please watch over us."

> "Forrest—Asher is waiting to see you in heaven."

> "Molson—My guardian angel. Miss you and love
> you."

> "Caro Charlito—The sheer abandonment of your
> smile was surpassed only by that of your heart.
> We'll always remember you. We will miss you."

After this we go off in separate directions, reading silently and looking at photographs, until I come across a photo that for me obscures all others. I'm unable to move, unable to divert my gaze. The subject in the photo is so familiar, yet the image takes me completely by surprise. I'm not thinking about her in the seconds before my eyes zoom in on the picture of the look-alike dog—honey colored, short-haired, long thin tail turned upward, stand-up ears so long that the tips bend forward, pulled downward by gravity—but once I see it I can think of nothing *but* her: Comet, my heart dog.

I remember so clearly the moment in which I fully understood the depth of my love for her, its absoluteness and completeness. It was a Sunday afternoon in the early 1980s, about four months after I'd coaxed her out of the middle of a busy street in Brookline and brought her home with me. My attempts to discover where she belonged turned up nothing, and she got a new name and a forever home with me and—until our relationship ended two years later—my partner Lenore.

On this particular afternoon in late summer, Lenore and I were having a lazy, meandering conversation about nothing of significance—until she asked me a question.

"If the house was on fire and you had to choose between saving William or Comet, who would you save?"

William was Lenore's eleven-month-old nephew.

I was shocked by her question, couldn't imagine what would prompt her to ask it.

"That's an impossible question."

"What do you mean it's an impossible question?"

"I mean that it would be impossible to choose. I really love William."

"So you'd save William."

"No. I'd save them both."

"You can't save them both—you can only save one of them."

The inside of my mouth became dry, and the muscles in my upper back turned tight and achy.

"But I'd *try* to save both of them."

"You *can't*—you have to choose."

My heart pounded against my ribcage, my breathing quickened. I couldn't imagine a more horrifying scenario. How could I choose one life over another? Where was it written that one species is of greater value than the rest of creation, and by virtue of what? I didn't know, couldn't remember.

"Why? Why do I have to save one and not the other?"

"Because I want to know who you'd choose if you had to."

And with that, I understood what was at the heart of the hypothetical situation she'd posed to me. It wasn't about William and Comet per se, nor was it about a fire. It was about me and her, about the kinds of reassurances sought in relationships. Lenore had become an aunt for the first time when William was born, and she was besotted with him. Her question to me was a test, coming from a place of needing to know we were in this together, that I shared her adoration of this child. And I did. What I didn't understand was why proof of my love for William had to come at the theoretical expense of a dog with whom I was equally besotted.

"Just because you want to know doesn't mean I have to choose. I'd save them both. End of conversation."

We didn't speak for several hours after that. And even though I knew Lenore would never force me to make this kind of choice if the situation were real, the conversation stuck with me, the scenario playing out over and over again in my mind—our beautiful 1800s Colonial farmhouse on fire, a baby and a dog trapped inside, me having to choose one life over another. But the continuously looping reel somehow never ended with me making a choice. When I approached the house, tried to see my way through the acrid and suffocating smoke, the scenario I'd created started over again. What was this about?

I watched the reel many more times that afternoon before I finally understood why it never ended. I wouldn't allow it to, couldn't face what I suspected in my heart would be my choice. Yes, it was all hypothetical, but I knew why I'd refused to answer Lenore's question. As difficult as it was for me to admit, even to myself, I simply couldn't find my way to what I knew most people would consider the correct response. If I'd allowed the scene to play out, it would almost certainly have shown me walking out of the house carrying Comet.

There was something terrifying about acknowledging this, about knowing the extent to which I'd be judged by most people were I to actually make that choice. The greater terror, though, came from a completely different place, from the realization that I loved so deeply and entirely a being who'd share my life for such a short period of time. I felt a pang of jealousy toward Lenore. If all went as it was supposed to, she'd have William for the rest of her life. But even if all went perfectly for Comet, I'd have her for no more than another fifteen years. Still, I reminded myself, I wasn't one hundred percent sure what choice I'd make if the house was really on fire. Perhaps terror was unnecessary.

Whatever lingering doubt I may have had regarding this matter was forever erased when, a couple of years later, I found myself in a real-life version of Lenore's hypothetical situation, a trial not by fire this time, but by ice.

It was a Saturday afternoon, and I'd taken Comet and Nike for a walk in Norris Park, a tract of conservation land on the South Shore that led down to the North River and was one of our favorite places to walk. Still only early March, it was cold enough for the pond near the entrance to appear frozen, but warm enough for that appearance to be deceiving. Somehow that fact, something every New Englander knows about late winter-early spring, didn't register with me as we walked past the pond on the way into the woods.

When we reached the trail, I let both dogs off-leash. We spent nearly an hour walking the peaceful paths, the dogs just ahead of me, never out of sight. As the pond came back into view I called to them. This was where I leashed them again, always, and they knew the drill. But on this day, for whatever reason, instead of coming when called they both took off in the opposite direction, straight for the pond.

I ran after them, and by the time I caught up both were out on the frozen water. Comet hadn't gone far, but Nike had almost reached the middle of the pond.

"C'mon, girls, let's go . . ."

They wagged their tails and began to make their way back across the ice toward me. Comet arrived safely, but Nike was still about fifty feet from shore, picking her way carefully across the slippery surface. I had just bent down to hook Comet up to her leash when I heard the splash, and in the split second it took me to look up I saw Nike go under. I screamed, long and loud enough to attract the attention of an elderly couple who stopped to help. I threw Comet's leash at the man, then ran along the edge of the pond calling to Nike, telling her I'd be right there, that she'd be okay.

As I looked for the fastest entry point, I could hear the couple yelling at me, begging me not to go out onto the ice.

Nike weighed less than I, so it shouldn't have been difficult to understand why my going out to rescue her was putting my own life at risk. But the couples' pleas had no more effect on me than if they'd been spoken in an incomprehensible language.

I watched Nike struggle to pull herself out of the frigid water, saw her head go back under, and knew that for me to remain on the shore and do nothing would be impossible. Could any parent stand by and allow their child to drown? In my mind it was no different, the instinct to save her life greater than even the primal instinct to preserve my own. Whatever powers in the universe had brought my dogs to me had, in doing so, chosen me as the steward of their lives. I refused to let one of those lives be snuffed out by something like this, by a situation I had the ability to change.

I stepped out onto the frozen pond, my eyes seeing nothing but Nike, my body powered by adrenaline. I'd taken no more than a few steps when, as if propelled by some unseen force beneath the water, Nike heaved herself out of the jagged hole. Cold, wet, and frightened, she skidded across the ice to where I stood. I grabbed her collar and held on tightly as we took the last few steps to safety. Then I leashed her, wrapped her tightly in my arms, and fell apart.

On the way home, I thought back to that hypothetical situation Lenore had posed. I'd never been absolutely sure of the choice I'd make if faced with an actual situation in which I had to choose between one life and another. Now I was.

The sudden sound of Marisel's voice startles me out of the past.

"Did you read this?"

I don't need to turn around to know where she is. I can tell from the choked sound of her voice that she's reading the remembrance letter written for the shelter dog. I walk over to her and put my arm around her.

"I did. And it absolutely broke my heart. But in a way, that letter was what helped put it back together again."

"What do you mean?"

At first I don't understand why she's asking me this question—didn't I just explain it all to her yesterday? But then I realize that in my excitement to describe the Dog Chapel to her, I'd forgotten to tell her about my encounter with Annie. It's such a startling omission, and so unlike me, that I wonder if perhaps I unconsciously chose to hold the memory safely within myself for just a while longer. I recount the entire story now. Marisel is quiet for what seems an eternity, and I wonder if she thinks I've finally and irrevocably lost my mind. But when she speaks, it's clear she believes I'm quite sane.

"This is a special place. It's very spiritual, and I'm not surprised that happened to you here. Not at all."

I reach for her hand and squeeze it. We're quiet for a moment and then she turns to me.

"Pea? I'm really glad we came here, but honestly? I think I've had enough for one day."

As I stand in front of the shelter dog's remembrance letter and photograph, I feel the familiar tightening of my throat. I've had enough for one day, too. We walk out of the Dog Chapel and head toward the parking lot in silence. As we approach the gallery, though, I feel a strong desire to go inside, and ask her if she feels up to it.

"Okay, but just for a few minutes."

The two-room gallery is filled with giclees, carvings, and furniture, but I decide to wait for another visit to absorb them. Instead, I focus my attention on a table of books. Most are children's books starring a black lab named Sally, but the book I'm drawn to has a print of the Dog Chapel bathed in golden light on its cover. It's titled *The Dog Chapel*, and its pages contain the story of the Dog Chapel and a collection of Huneck's art. A quick transaction at the register, and we're out the door, headed home again.

As Marisel maneuvers slowly and carefully down the bumpy dirt road, the Jeep finds its way in and out of ruts and potholes, rocking me gently back and forth in a way I find surprisingly soothing.

Neither of us speaks. The weight of words is just too heavy. Our silence doesn't bother me. It's a comfortable silence, the kind that comes from having known someone for a very long time. Marisel reaches for my hand and holds it, and I lean over and kiss her cheek. In these two gestures lie all that needs saying.

BACK AT THE house, I sit perched on the window seat in the sun room just off the kitchen, reading the Dog Chapel book while Marisel bustles around a few feet away preparing lunch.

I learn that a couple of years before building the Dog Chapel, Stephen Huneck had almost died from Adult Respiratory Distress Syndrome. No one thought he was going to make it except his wife Gwen. He was in a coma for two weeks, and when he finally emerged from it he had to learn to walk again. His dogs literally stayed by his side during this phase of his recovery, walking on either side of him, the way dogs do when their puppies are first learning to navigate their world.

Not long after he was discharged from the hospital and had settled in at home, he had what he described as a wild idea, something he became obsessed with—the idea to build a chapel on Dog Mountain. He wanted the chapel to be a place where the spiritual bonds between people and their dogs were celebrated, a place open to dogs and where people of all faiths and beliefs would feel welcome. As I continue to read, I'm amazed at the extent to which he was able to execute his artistic vision. It's everything he imagined, right down to the very last detail—the white steeple with the winged gold Lab on top, the light filtering into the sanctuary through the stained-glass windows, dog carvings everywhere, soul-opening music playing. Small wonder he considers the Dog Chapel his greatest work of art.

I turn back to the book's dedication, and am touched to see that *The Dog Chapel* is for the Hunecks' dog Sally, the black Lab whose likeness I'd seen on the cover of all those books in the gallery. She'd died suddenly and unexpectedly, I read, and at the age of eleven, leaving Huneck heartbroken but firm in his belief that in their hearts and souls, they'd remain together.

I close the book softly, reverentially. He gets it. He understands what it is to have one's heart broken by loving and losing a dog. But it's more than that—he also understands that a chapel, even one as unorthodox as the Dog Chapel, is a place of faith, a place in which to express the belief that those we love will always be with us, that we will see them again one day. And because he knows these things, the Dog Chapel has become a place not only in which to celebrate the spiritual bonds we have with our dogs, but to grieve their loss as well. I say a silent prayer of gratitude for the heart and mind and artistic gifts of this remarkable man, and then turn to the business of lunch.

THREE

I'M ALWAYS AMAZED at the extent to which a simple word, a single diagnosis, can come to define, for a time, a family's existence. For some families the word is cancer, for some it's depression, for others it's addiction. For my family, the word is dementia. My grandmother had it. My father-in-law had it. My dog Comet had it. And several years after that first visit to the Dog Chapel, Chispa begins to exhibit signs of it, too. But for reasons it will take me a long time to understand, I'm unable to recognize those signs and symptoms for what they are. Instead, I persist for nearly eighteen months after their first appearance in believing that what's wrong with my dog is nothing more than a very bad case of anxiety—an anxiety gone completely haywire. And it's an easy thing to settle into, this misguided belief, because all I know of canine dementia is Comet's experience, twelve years earlier.

FOR COMET, DEMENTIA creeps up slowly, silently, taking little bits of her memory and cognitive abilities at a time. First she loses the ability to perceive depth. In a surreal moment, I watch in disbelief as she walks off the stairwell ledge in our third-floor converted attic bedroom in the house in Chelsea, landing one floor below. Even now, my gut goes into free-fall right along with her body every time I think of it. The area of the floor where she lands is carpeted and she's more shaken than hurt, but it's a defining moment—the moment I realize the extent to which she's no longer herself.

Other symptoms follow. She becomes stuck in corners, rambles from room to room during the day, and wanders around the bedroom at night, unable to find her way back to her bed. Marisel builds a railing around the stairwell ledge to prevent future falls, but I obsess about the multitude of other things that might happen to Comet—things like getting stuck behind the sink or toilet in the tiny en-suite half-bath, or falling asleep standing up in a corner because she can't remember how to turn around. I can't bear the thought of her finding herself in these situations, so I stay awake at night to make sure they don't occur.

When she goes outside she no longer sniffs around the grass or the borders of the flower beds. Instead she walks up and down the driveway in a straight line, seemingly without purpose or interest. When she reaches the fence at one end she turns around and walks the length of the long driveway again, until she reaches the fence at the other end. She repeats the same pattern, as if caught in a time warp, until I tell her it's time to go back inside and she follows me up the porch stairs and into the house.

I wonder how she experiences this new state of being. Are her circumscribed travels along the driveway perhaps as fascinating to her now as her previous explorations of every scent held in grass and soil had once been? Or does she miss her old self, her former habits and delights? When she looks at me now her eyes often seem empty, and I wonder if she knows who I am, or even who she herself is.

I take her to her vet Bari, hoping for some concrete advice as to what's going on inside my dog's head. And this is the first thing I come to understand about canine dementia—no one, including the person most familiar from a medical perspective with Comet's aging body, can really know what's happening in her brain, or provide any significant insight into the extent to which she understands her relationship to home, to self, to me.

It's maddening.

I bring Comet to my friend Donna, the vet who treated her when I lived on the South Shore and for many years after I moved to the city. I'm hoping for a different answer to my questions, but Donna tells me essentially the same thing as Bari. And they both tell me something else: Comet isn't in physical pain, and as long as I can tolerate the fact that she's not the same dog she once was, there's no need to put her down.

So we go on like this, the disease taking a little more of her awareness here, a little more of her memory there, and I continue to love her as ferociously and completely as one being can love another.

One Saturday in early October, I decide to take her to Norris Park. It's a day of nearly unbearable clarity and beauty, the kind of day that's almost heartbreaking in its perfection. The sky is a shade of blue that usually appears in southern New England only in the fall, a blue mixed with light and depth, a blue so intense and exuberant it swallows you whole.

The sun is warm that day in Norris Park, the fall air infused with a touch of late summer. I pull up to the entrance and park the car. Comet is older and frailer than when we last were here, the dementia having more and more of an effect. She's always loved these woods, and I know this will probably be the last time she'll ever walk down the familiar path—the pond up the way a bit on the left, one of the mud holes she loves to wade in just slightly further on the right, the sounds of the living forest everywhere, piquing her curiosity.

I get out of the car and open the passenger door. A year ago, Comet would have leapt out and headed straight for the woods, unable to wait one second longer, even for me. This day is different. She lifts her nose into the air and sniffs, making no attempt to jump from the car. I pick her up off the seat and place her gently on the ground. She stands there quietly, and I tell myself I'd give anything—absolutely anything—to be trying to grab onto the end of her leash as she bounds past me into the woods.

"C'mon, sweet girl, let's go."

She obediently walks along beside me, and I wonder what she's thinking, wonder if she has any idea where we are. We slowly make our way out of the parking area, her arthritis dictating our pace. As we enter the woods, the air smells of moist earth and fresh pine. I inhale deeply, the co-mingling scents stirring some primeval nerve buried within me. We walk along the path, its surface slippery with fallen, dried out pine needles accumulated from seasons past, until the pond appears just around the bend. The pond's still waters reflect the cloudless blue sky and the red, orange, and yellow leaves of the trees bordering its banks as clearly as if the reflection were a photograph.

We take a few steps over to the pond and stop at the water's edge. Comet stands quietly beside me, still on leash. I gaze down into the water and see a middle-aged woman and an elderly dog, whose thirteen years together have included a multitude of incarnations of the love, joy, change and sorrow that comprise life. And then, for one brief moment, I see our future in that reflection. It's as if an acorn has fallen from a tree into the water, causing the reflected image of our present to blur and alter itself. In the reconfigured version of our reflection I stand by the pond alone, holding a leash attached to nothing.

I back away from the water, unable to face this vision of our future. I will instead immerse myself in the present, in the beauty of this glorious New England fall day, and will be grateful for the time I've been given with Comet—even while knowing that another fifty years with her would still not be enough.

As we head away from the pond and into the woods, I release the clasp of the leash from her collar. I expect her to continue to walk slowly along beside me, and for a while she does. But suddenly, as if some dormant sensory memory has been awakened, she begins to trot ahead of me, nose to the ground.

What is she thinking? Does she have specific memories of this place, memories that include me, Nike, or perhaps my father, who has often accompanied me and the dogs on our walks here? Or is her reaction something more visceral, triggered by the sounds and smells of the woods? I have no way of knowing, am only happy to see her step quicken.

We walk along in this way for a time, Comet just a bit ahead of me. I watch for signs that she's tiring, begin to wonder if we should turn back. But she moves forward with an energy I haven't seen in many months, nose sniffing the ground and every so often the air, tail high, ears pointed straight up in alert mode. I decide to continue on.

A bit further along the path we come to a clearing in the woods, a place where the marshland of the North River comes into view. Beyond this spot, up to the right, the river itself is visible, the reflection of sun on dark blue water sending bursts of light spinning, like tiny frenetic ballerinas dancing over the current. We continue on past the marsh, back into the woods, and along to another clearing, where a weathered gray wooden dock and boat house sit further out over the marsh.

My father has often seen a kingfisher sitting on the dock's railings, and I look over at the dock, hoping to see the bird myself. But today the railings are empty, and we move on. At this point the path takes a slightly uphill turn, and I again begin to worry about Comet. I stop for a moment to let her walk ahead of me, to watch for signs that she's tiring. But her pace is steady, briskly efficient.

Where is this energy coming from? How long will it continue? I doubt that even she knows. But I wonder if perhaps, somehow, she knows something else—knows that this will be the final time she walks in these woods. The path ahead of me blurs as tears materialize out of nowhere. Our life together is being lived on borrowed time now—borrowed from age, physical debilitation, and a hateful disease. Does she know this in the same way I do? I realize it doesn't matter. What matters is that today, there is the unexpected gift of her amazing energy, propelling her forward through the woods she loves, allowing her to experience once again what it is to be a dog, what it is to be herself.

As I stand watching her, she suddenly senses I'm no longer right behind her. She stops and looks over her shoulder, then trots back to stand next to me, tail wagging. I know right then that in the entirety of my lifetime there will be no moment more perfect in its fragility than this one, this moment in which I stand beside this dog—the one for whom I'd give up everything—in a place so beloved, on an unexpectedly warm fall afternoon, marveling at the way in which time has somehow reversed itself.

We continue up the path. Comet has slowed her pace and now walks beside me, tail held up, the tip arched over her back in its familiar indicator of happiness. Seeing the way in which she holds her tail, the apparent ease with which she's made the walk, I begin to indulge in magical thinking—wondering if, perhaps, bringing her here might have actually changed things . . . might have set right all that's wrong with her, might have somehow enabled this inexplicable reversal of time.

As we approach the mud hole she and Nike have spent so many satisfying moments wading through, I wonder what she'll do. From a practical perspective I hope she won't roll in it; I've forgotten to bring a post-mud-roll towel. But there's a part of me that wants her to wade in as far as she can—until she finds the place where the mud is the thickest, wettest, and messiest—then roll on her back, tail moving back and forth like a slender rudder, until she's covered with the stuff. Because if she does that, she just might live forever.

But she seems oblivious to the mud hole's existence, walks right past it without even a glance.

When we reach the point in the path where our loop reconnects with the main path, I notice she's beginning to tire. She drops behind me and I stop, wait for her to catch up, then slow my pace to match hers. We pass the brook on the left and, further up, the peculiar old granite wheels that lie in a grassy clearing off to the right, their purpose unapparent. Comet has clocked a lot of time sniffing those wheels, perhaps as puzzled by their presence as I've always been, but today their scent holds no interest for her.

As we round the final bend, the one that will take us out of the woods and to the parking lot, I don't want to leave. I want to go back and do it all over again, want to spend eternity walking that same looped path in the woods with her at my side. For this, no bargain with any devil would be unacceptable.

We approach the pond once more, but this time we pass it by. I'm grateful she doesn't want to walk down to the water's edge again. Her choice spares me the agony of seeing our reflection in the pond one last time.

When we reach the parking lot she heads directly to the car. I open the passenger door and lift her onto the seat, then bend down to kiss her slender head, the smell of her a mix of sun, fresh air, and pine. Inhaling her scent, I wonder, for at least the hundredth time, what forces aligned within the universe to enable our paths to cross all those years ago on that street corner in Brookline. My life would have been so diminished without that moment, without her.

I shut the car door, walk around to the driver's side, and settle myself behind the wheel. I glance over at my beautiful girl, her gray muzzle resting on her front paws, and see that she has already fallen asleep. I back the car out of its space and stop for one last look at the woods beyond before I drive away.

Fall turns to winter, and then one day she's gone. Just like that, unexpectedly and silently—as silent as the disease that robbed her of so much of who she'd been, yet capriciously saw fit, on a perfect fall afternoon in Norris Park, to give her back to herself and to me, if only for a very short time.

WITH CHISPA IT'S different. The disease isn't silent at all; it's loud and frantic. As the months pass, she experiences her usual anxiety triggers—fireworks, thunderstorms, watching me and Marisel leave for work in the morning—as even more distressing. The whining and panting I've long ago come to consider normal reactions to the things that make her anxious evolve into loud, shrill, panicked barking. Because these symptoms aren't at all what I believe canine dementia to be, I assume Chispa is suffering from a generalized anxiety that's clearly reaching a crisis point.

I bring her to see Bari, who by this time has become the family vet. We discuss various options for treating anxiety, and the potential benefits and side effects of each. In the end, I decide to begin with some non-pharmaceutical remedies. Although I have no way of knowing it now, this decision will later come to haunt me.

The next morning I turn on the classical music station before leaving for work, then stop at Whole Foods to buy a bottle of Composure, an herbal tincture recommended for calming anxious dogs. The combination of music and Composure seems to work well. I'm elated, but my joy is as short-lived as the tincture's effects.

Chispa's symptoms re-emerge in less than a week, the barking worse than before. I increase her dose of Composure, turn up the volume on the radio, and install air conditioners in the windows to muffle the ordinary, outside noises that fuel her anxiety. Nothing seems to help for more than a couple of days. I understand now that these measures are essentially the equivalent of placing band-aids on a broken leg. Chispa's anxiety appears to respond to nothing, and I begin to re-think the non-pharmaceutical route to getting things under control.

One day in the midst of all this, Marisel and I decide to drive up to New Hampshire for the weekend. I want to take Chispa and Laika to the Dog Chapel, and I feel the need to take myself there as well. Chispa's continuous state of distress and my inability to do anything to alleviate it has taken an emotional toll on me, and I crave the sense of peace and comfort I experience in the Dog Chapel.

On Sunday morning we drive from Littleton to St. Johnsbury. It's winter, the mountain air cold and dry. When we arrive at the chapel's parking area it's empty, and I'm happy to have the chapel to ourselves for at least a little while. We walk into the sanctuary and sit in the pew furthest from the vestibule, right up front. The chapel is unheated, and I watch as our collective breath forms four little clouds that dissipate into the air, leaving a part of each of us to be absorbed into the open space of the sanctuary.

Laika sits next to me on the floor, and I run my hand over her soft, dense fur. In the past few months her arthritis has become more painful and debilitating, and here in the Dog Chapel I pray for her comfort. As I pray, I envision a warm, golden light emanating from my hand into her old and achy joints, easing their movement and lessening her pain. I see her joints becoming warm and loose and flexible, and picture her rising effortlessly from the floor. I hold that vision for some time, then open my eyes and look over at Marisel.

"Can we change places? I want to sit next to Chispa for a few minutes."

She gets up and we switch sides. Chispa is whining softly, but quiets down when I touch her.

"Good girl . . . you're a good girl."

I place my hands gently on top of her head and imagine the same golden light I'd visualized for Laika entering Chispa's brain, turning her anxiety into a state of complete calm. I envision her lying on the couch at home, quiet and happy, interested in her world. I see the light that had once been in her eyes shine as she looks at me, the frightened, bewildered look that's now often there gone. It's this last vision that I hold in my mind as my hands hover over her head—the light in her eyes that tells me she's herself.

I release the vision, sending it out into the Dog Chapel as a kind of virtual picture, to join the other pictures of dogs at their happiest and healthiest posted on the walls. I open my eyes, put my gloves back on, shove my painfully cold hands into my coat pockets, and get up.

"I think I'm going to walk around for a few minutes and read some of the notes."

"Okay. I'm going to take the dogs and go wait for you in the Jeep."

I watch them leave, and hope that my silent prayers will be heard, my visions actualized. I believe in the possibility of miracles, and a miracle for my aging and ailing dogs is more likely to happen here, I think, than anywhere else on the planet. I walk a few feet to the front end of the chapel. My exploration of the Dog Chapel up to this point has centered on the vestibule and the sanctuary's back wall, and I'm curious to see what I might find in a different section of the chapel.

I begin on the left side of the wall, walking slowly, searching for the notes that will speak to me. Maybe it's the numbing cold, but I'm having a hard time focusing on the words and pictures laid out in kaleidoscopic patterns before me.

Then, about midway along the wall, I find one that penetrates.

> "Maddy—A gentle spirit, a loving friend, a soul that will always be missed and forever remembered. You touched the lives of all those around you. Run now—bark, play, chase, be happy. We love you."

As I read the words left behind by Maddy's people, my heart aches. Maddy is, in a sense, Everydog. She has lived and died, and in the space between her birth and death has graced everyone who knew her with what is perhaps a dog's greatest gift to humankind—unconditional, non-judgmental love. The kind of love that's impossible to replicate in most human relationships, but that most humans are in deep and desperate need of. The kind of love that shapes you, changes you, frequently astonishes you, and weaves itself so tightly into your individual fabric that it becomes a permanent part of you. The kind of love that when lost in its visible, earthly form, leads to a grief so jagged, so intense, it takes your breath away.

Standing in the Dog Chapel now, in the silent company of the hundreds of thousands of words that have been strung together from this place of suffocating grief, I marvel at the resilience of the human spirit. But most of all, I stand in utter amazement at the ways in which the love between people and their dogs endures, in life, through death, and beyond.

FOUR

ON THE RIDE back to Littleton I can't get Maddy out of my mind, can't stop thinking about the depth of my love for Chispa and Laika, for Comet and Nike—that limitless love spoken of in the Dog Chapel, a love incapable of being contained by boundaries of time or space, life or death, a love as essential to me as the air I breathe. Reflecting on that love now, on what it means to me, on the place it has in my life and in the order of things, I'm surprised a bit by my need for it. Growing up, I was one of the lucky ones, raised by good parents who loved me unconditionally. Why, then, has a dog's unconditional love been so transformative? Where did the need for this particular type of love begin?

An image of my six-year-old self comes into focus. I'm sitting on an old, ornate wooden settee in the garden courtyard of my grandparents' house in Guayaquil, Ecuador, where my family had recently moved. The expression on my face is solemn. I am silent and mostly still, my only movement the rhythmic passing of my hand along the body of the small, equally silent white dog leaning against me. Cachita, my grandfather's dog.

CACHITA THEORETICALLY BELONGED to both my grandparents, but in reality she was my grandfather's dog. Her choice, not his, but one I'm sure he was delighted by. Up until then I'd never lived with a dog, had no idea a dog could be friend, sibling, and even parent to a lonely and homesick girl. As a small child in a house where most people spoke very little if any English, my inability to communicate was jarring and isolating, and I longed to be back home in Rhode Island, where everything was familiar and my best friend lived right next door.

In Ecuador I didn't have any friends, not for a long while. And so it was Cachita I turned to, Cachita who became my friend, the friend I looked forward to seeing after school, to telling about my day—my real day, not the day I made up to tell my parents—and to sitting with when I was lonely. It was from this place of loneliness that my need for the silent, unquestioning love a dog offers took root. In the presence of Cachita I felt validated, believed I was good and kind and worthy of being loved, of being chosen as a friend. There was nothing wrong with me. Cachita had accepted me, hadn't she? The reason I was left on the outside of things at school had nothing to do with me, with who I was.

By this time I understood some of the human emotions that get in the way of love—jealousy, fear, anger. I understood, too, that dogs have similar emotions. Cachita was sometimes frightened when a pair of hands reached down too quickly to pick her up, sometimes jealous when my grandfather's time and attention were directed elsewhere when she wanted them for herself. Whether frightened or jealous, her reaction was the same, a low growl and a quick nip.

Still, her emotions seemed so much less complicated than a human's, so much purer and closer to the surface. Maybe this was why her fear and jealousy didn't prevent her from loving. They were simply feelings, unattached to or supported by thoughts. It was as if Cachita's emotions, once expressed, were immediately forgotten, replaced once more with a dog's simple, transparent desire to give and receive love.

It wasn't long before I became dependent on Cachita, on this immediate, no words necessary, no-matter-what love she offered me, on the positive way it made me feel about myself. When we finally moved out of my grandparents' home and into our own house hours away, a house near the beach and complete with a new best friend right next door, even then I missed her terribly.

I DIDN'T THINK much about a dog's unique way of expressing unconditional love until many years later. I was in my twenties, in therapy, having difficulties with love. I couldn't seem to find a healthy relationship, and when I finally did, couldn't make it last. I wanted that truly, madly, deeply kind of love, and I wanted it to be offered unconditionally. But maybe I only thought this was what I wanted, because instead of embracing those who loved me I pushed them away.

It would take years of work before I'd begin to understand why I wouldn't let anyone into the deep places, why I sometimes found it difficult to believe in even my parents' unwavering love. Before I could build and sustain the kind of relationship I wanted, I had to love myself in that deep and unconditional way first. But I couldn't, didn't know how. I'd known once, back in Guayaquil. But so much had happened since then, so much beyond my ability to grasp and process, so much beyond the ability of even good and loving parents to control.

The summer we returned home from Ecuador I was seven, once again uprooted and lonely. We spent that summer on a small island with a grand total of four homes on it, two of which were vacant at the time. There were no children my age on the island, so I made friends with the only other person living there, an elderly gentleman who'd known my family for years. But his interest in me was distorted by his own experience of loneliness, and his attentions left me confused, feeling complicit in something I sensed was wrong. At the time I didn't possess the words to articulate why it was wrong, and I never spoke of it until well into adulthood.

What I took away from that experience all those years ago was the belief that I was somehow not a good person, not worthy of real love. By the time I was able to understand that the personality defect lay within him and wasn't mine to own, this negative self-image had already taken root, sinking deeper and deeper until I no longer saw it, no longer thought about it.

RELEASING THAT BELIEF has been one of the most difficult things I've ever attempted to do. The intellectual work of learning to rethink and reframe the events of my seventh summer has been done, but the necessary heart work is on-going, done in the loving and non-judgmental company of my dogs. It's an enlightening and frustrating process, an odd blend of learning and unlearning, the desired result like quicksilver—within my grasp one minute, only to be lost the next. But my attempts to unlearn the past move forward, remain constant, as does the unconditional and healing love my dogs offer me in every moment of their existence, and even beyond.

So many of the notes in the Dog Chapel speak of a dog's unconditional love, and I find myself wondering about the ways in which others have been healed by it. To live, I think, is to be among the walking wounded, to bear the scars of old injuries, to live with the pain of hurts that have become chronic over a lifetime of neglect. What wounds did Maddy heal for her family during her life with them? What changes did Butter and Bonnye see their person through, what happened during the dark childhood nights Ruby's person mentions, and how did a dog's love make those nights feel just a bit safer, a bit more bearable?

I have no way of knowing the answers; can only imagine what they might be. But beyond those questions lies a larger one: How do dogs manage, without benefit of shared language, to access and heal the kinds of deep hurts that exist within those they love? I find this fascinating, the kind of question with an answer so simple, yet so amazing. The simple part of the answer is, "They love me with their whole heart, just as I am, no matter what I do or what I've done." The amazing part is, "They don't know how to love in any other way." It's a dangerous way to love, one that leaves a dog vulnerable to great sadness. I learned this truth from a shelter dog years ago, a dog who taught me that which he himself would never understand.

WHEN I ARRIVED for my first volunteer shift at the Northeast Animal Shelter, a dog whose run had a note on it caught my eye. The note told potential adopters that he was eight years old, left there because his family had moved away and couldn't take him with them. I wondered what this dog must be thinking, imagined the grief and loneliness he must feel at having been separated from the people he loved and considered his pack. Did he wonder, in whatever way a dog might, if he'd somehow been unworthy of love? I felt an immediate kinship with this dog and asked a staff member if I could take him for a walk. Yes, I was told, please do; he's having a hard time here.

I walked out of the shelter and up the street with him, then climbed a small hill. When we reached the top we sat down next to one another, bodies touching, a temporary pack of two. I wrapped my arm tightly around him, trying to undo the hurt even while knowing I couldn't.

So instead I talked, tried to heal rather than undo. The irony of it didn't escape me, my way of expressing love so different from his. Still, though my words meant nothing to him, I hoped that the touch of my hand and the tone of my voice would reach his wounded places, in the same way that my dogs' silent presence had never failed to reach those places within me, in the same way I was certain his own silent presence had reached those places within the people he loved.

I told him he was good, and beautiful, and that none of what had happened was his fault. And I told him that even though it might not seem like it right now, his family had loved him, loved him enough to bring him to a no-kill shelter, loved him enough to give him a second chance at finding a forever family. And when I was talked out, we just sat together on the hill in the afternoon sunlight. I wanted so much to adopt him myself, but knew we already had a full house. So I did the only thing I could do for him—kept him with me on the warm hillside until my volunteer shift was almost over.

It was nearly two hours before we returned to the shelter, and it broke my heart to have to leave him. I thought about him all the way home, couldn't get him out of my mind for the entirety of the week before my next shift. When I arrived again at the shelter, I was assigned the task of hosing down some of the outside runs. I finished the job quickly, anxious to go check on him, convinced he wouldn't be there.

But he was, the despondency in his eyes so heart wrenching that it took every bit of self-control I possessed not to adopt him right then and there. I wanted to, as desperately as he wanted a home, but it simply wasn't an option. And so we walked back up the hillside, sat together in the sun again for the rest of my shift. At some point during the next two hours I knew I wouldn't see him the following week. The shelter didn't know it yet, but this would be my last day as a volunteer. I'd had no idea what I was signing up for; the emotional pain was just too much for me. I was grateful for those who could handle it, but I wasn't one of them.

I was sure he'd be adopted by a wonderful family in the end, but it wasn't just about him. There'd be more, week after week, dogs who'd loved their people and were miserable without them, who grieved the loss of those people as deeply as I grieved the loss of my dogs. As disappointed as I was in myself for not being able to follow through with my commitment to the shelter, I simply didn't have it in me to bear continual witness to such sadness.

LOVING THE WAY dogs love takes courage, but they don't know it. It's just what they do, who they are. But I understand the implications of loving in this way and know how terrifying it can be to love a person no matter what, how great the chances of not being loved unconditionally in return. Yet I've never once worried about this with my dogs, as I've always known that my unequivocal love for them is returned. Loving and being loved by them has made me braver about love, more willing to take the risk for having seen the pure bliss that can come of it.

There's a Huneck print in the Dog Chapel book that reminds me of the way my dogs' love makes me feel. It's a rendering of a Dalmation and a man, the man's face unseen. In his hand he holds a mirror, the glass facing the dog. As she looks into it, she sees reflected back at her the letters G-O-D, spelled out in a Dalmation's black spots. It's my favorite print in the book, the one that speaks most deeply to all that I know to be true about dogs, especially my own.

When I look at my dogs I see so much of what I myself aspire to be—deeply contented, at peace with myself and the world around me, forgiving, joyful. And in the silent spaces that happen in a relationship with a dog, I've seen something else. I've seen the love of God.

The long, comfortable spells of silence my dogs have provided me remind me in some ways of other silent spaces in which I often search for and encounter God. An empty church, an underwater reef, a deserted cemetery, a mountain top, a trail deep in the woods, the night sky. I've found God in each of these places, sometimes once, sometimes over and over again. But I've never experienced God's love with any greater clarity than when I've looked with silence into the eyes of one of my dogs and gazed into her soul.

I've always been told God is love, unconditional love, and if this is true, then loving and being loved by a dog must surely be one of God's ways of providing a direct pathway to divine love, right here on earth. When my dogs die, and the direct pathway to that love is no longer accessible to me, the loss of it, along with the loss of the unique being that was my dog, is devastating.

And so I hold onto it the only way I can, in my heart, in my memory. I hold onto it forever, even though I know I'll eventually bring another dog into my home, another dog who'll provide that link to unconditional and healing love. And I hold onto it because I know the new pathway will be different from the ones before it, just as the dog providing it will be, and I want the lessons each of my dogs have taught me about unconditional love to remain a part of me. Holding a dog's love close, even when that dog is no longer physically with me, is what enables that love to be forever, allows it to transcend all boundaries, and eventually transforms the kind of grief that brings people to the Dog Chapel into something hopeful, reassuring, and comforting.

The Word of Dog
LOVE

"Sam—I saved you from the shelter. You saved me from believing love was impossible."

"Lucy—We love you and you are missed more than you can ever know. May the breeze always be at your face . . ."

"I had loved other animals before but this was different. I was in love with this dog. His loss taught me that we can grieve just as deeply for our animal "loves" as for our human ones; that we are all connected, that there is no break in the ties that bind us. That the love energy does not dissipate. And no matter where we go he is always there. There isn't a day that passes that I don't think of him and my sadness turns to gratitude for having loved and been loved so unconditionally."

"Sadie & Sarah—I rescued you and you spent the rest of your lives giving me love and comfort. I will always miss and love you."

"For all the dogs I've loved, and all the dogs yet to guide me on this journey . . . thank you."

"Nook—You were always loved. Sorry we didn't find your body sooner."

"We love you and miss you, Sam. May your spirit run free and joyous."

"Norris—I will always remember my "first love/ dog"—you were the perfect companion—I have so many happy memories of you—hope you are still chasing Frisbees in heaven."

"Mozart, you were a wonderful dog—thoughtful, considerate, intuitive, and above all loving. You saved my mom's life and made mine easier to accept. I miss you all the time. I hope you have all the ice cream you want in dog heaven."

"Snoopy: I still have the brown couch & I still see you on it from time to time. You're not to be forgotten. I will always love you."

"For my beloved dog Sam—Thank you for being the best dog I could of ever wanted. I will never forget when we got you from the shelter how happy you were and you even doggy smiled. I will never forget all the times we had together, from taking long rides in the car to the many hikes we took. But the day finally came that we had to say goodbye to each other. It was the hardest day of my life. But you let me know it was your time. I know most people would think that day would make me cry. But actually I'm so thankfull. Because in your very special way you made it easy. I will always love you. Your forever owner."

"Dear Griz, It's been 4 years that I lost you, but it seems like yesterday. I never knew, imagined how difficult it would be. I now know that I will have a hole in my heart forever."

FIVE

NEARLY A YEAR after that wintry visit to the Dog Chapel, life as it was then is no longer.

Laika is gone. Losing her comes out of nowhere, in the spring, just a few months after I'd prayed over her in the chapel. It begins with a limp, the second time she's come up lame in less than two weeks. The first bout of lameness lasted only a day or so, but this time is different. In less than two days the lameness becomes so severe that navigating the stairs is impossible for her. There's no stairless way in or out of our house other than through the basement in-law apartment, where our close friend Edwin lives. So with Edwin's blessing, we move Laika downstairs to live with him until the lameness resolves itself.

But by day three it's clear the lameness is becoming worse. Not only that, but the lump we'd noticed about a week ago on her right hind leg—the lame leg—seems to be growing. We'd assumed the lump was just a bruise, caused by knocking into something. Why, then, wasn't it shrinking? We call Maija, the wonderful mobile vet we've recently begun using for routine care. She thinks Laika may need x-rays, which her mobile practice isn't equipped to do, so we call around and make the earliest appointment we can get—later that morning at a nearby veterinary clinic.

The vet who sees Laika is very kind, and takes his time with her. He positions himself on the floor beside her and examines her thoroughly, manipulating her right hind leg and rolling his fingers over the lump. He's gentle and she allows him to complete the examination, but the narrowing of her eyes reveals her pain. Finally, he stands up.

"I'd like to do some blood work and possibly an x-ray, if she can tolerate it. And I'd also like to aspirate that lump."

We agree to all of it, and he leads Laika out of the room. When they return, she immediately lies down and closes her eyes.

"I won't have the results until tomorrow. I decided against the x-rays. Let's see what the blood work and aspiration show first. For now, just try to keep her comfortable, keep her away from the stairs, and you can use a towel sling across her belly, right underneath her hind quarters, to help support her if walking becomes too hard for her."

We drive home and get Laika settled, then go upstairs to check on Chispa and call Maija. I relay the morning's events and our conversation with the clinic vet, and promise to call her when we get the lab results. The next morning, the clinic vet calls with devastating news. The lump on Laika's right hind leg isn't a bump. It's a mast cell tumor—an unusually aggressive tumor that's already begun releasing its toxic cells into her body, causing her lameness. Her prognosis is poor, and in his opinion we have two options: consider chemotherapy or put her down. I tell him we're not going to put a fourteen-year-old dog through chemo, and hang up. What else is there to say?

I call Maija, and she offers to come that day to examine Laika herself. I don't expect her to provide a different diagnosis, but find the idea of her hand and presence in this surreal situation comforting, stabilizing. Yes, I tell her. Please come.

When she arrives, Laika's leg is hot and swollen.

"I think what's probably happened is that some of the mast cells were released into her leg during the aspiration, which is what's causing the swelling. We can try her on some Benadryl and see if that'll reduce the inflammation and make her more comfortable."

I write down the proper Benadryl dosage and check the medicine cabinet to see if we have any on hand. We do, but the expiration date stamped on the bottom of the slender box has long since passed. We'll have to pick some up later. And then Maija asks us what we want to do, given our very limited options. From our perspective, there's really only one option, and we make an appointment for the following early afternoon to put Laika down. No more trips to the vet. Her final hours will be spent at home.

That night, while Edwin's at work, I lie sprawled lengthwise across his bed in the semi-darkness, the room illuminated only by a small St. Lazarus votive candle on the dresser, the same candle we lit for Laika the day she came up lame. St. Lazarus, whom Jesus raised from the dead. My arm dangles over the edge of the bed, hand resting on Laika's body, checking for the rhythm of her breathing. I'm terrified she'll leave us in the middle of the night, that she won't live until the next afternoon, when we'll all be with her to say goodbye. My fingertips brush rhythmically along her rib cage, skimming over her soft fur.

How can this—any of it—be happening?

"Please hang on sweetheart, just a little while longer. Please don't die alone . . ."

And she does hang on, for another sixteen hours, until Maija arrives the next afternoon. We decide to say goodbye to Laika in Edwin's apartment, the rooms as familiar to her as her own home upstairs, Edwin as beloved to her as Marisel and I.

Gathered on the floor around Laika's bed, we stroke her head, her back. We tell her how much we love her, how much she means to us. And then Maija leans over her, speaking calmly and lovingly, and the life-ending injection disappears into Laika's skin. Before our old girl has to endure one more minute of pain, she's gone. The flame in the St. Lazarus votive flickers, and then the votive itself explodes with a loud pop.

No one speaks until Maija asks what we want to do with Laika's body. We want her cremated, individually, her ashes returned to us in an urn.

"Okay. I'll take care of everything. I'm so sorry . . . she was a good girl. You did the right thing for her, but I know that doesn't make it any easier."

Maija wraps Laika in a blanket, then picks her up and carries her out to the car. She lays Laika's body down in an already-cleared space in the tailgate area, and I lean over my still-warm dog for one final kiss, one last opportunity to smell the fresh scent of her. And then I step away, knowing Laika's not in that body, not anymore.

We stand in the driveway until Maija's car turns the corner and disappears from view, then walk slowly back inside. It seems so impossible, the week's sequence of events. How can Laika, who'd seemed perfectly healthy six days ago, be gone? I can't make sense of any of it.

When Laika's ashes are returned to us, they're in an urn of polished Maplewood, with a space for a photograph on the front. Marisel and I select a picture of Laika swimming in our pond in Littleton, along with a small, scallop-edged piece of paper with a quote by Thoreau: "Always maintain a kind of summer, Even in the middle of winter." That—exactly that—was the essence of Laika.

Her death leaves me reeling. But there's more to deal with. The day before we put Laika down Chispa undergoes surgery to remove a small eyelid mass. The procedure itself is relatively simple, her recovery anything but. The anesthesia sets in motion a horrifying, heartbreaking ten-hour barking jag during which I truly believe both Chispa and I might lose our minds. Eventually she returns to a more normal state, but normal for her no longer fits any commonly accepted definition of the word and after exhaustive internet research on treatments for canine anxiety, I ask Bari to put her on Prozac.

And, after a long summer spent grieving for Laika, we adopt a Puerto Rican rescue dog through the Save a Sato program at the Northeast Animal Shelter in Salem. We hope the dog, a gentle whippet-Jack Russell terrier mix named Chula, will provide companionship for Chispa and bring joy and hope, which by then felt so long absent, back into our lives.

The fall months are happy ones for our reconfigured family. Chula's presence and energy bring new life to Chispa. As I watch my two girls playing in the yard, it's hard to believe Chispa is the same dog who just a few months ago could barely walk, or Chula the same dog who'd come to us recovering from surgery to mend a shattered hip. To me, it's nothing short of miraculous. As the days pass and all seems well, the painful tension that's become a fixture in my shoulders and upper back loosens. My shoulders return from somewhere around my ears to their proper position as I relax into our new reality, lulled by Chispa's improvement into believing that everything is now just fine.

But as the months pass and we ring in 2010, Chispa slips back into her anxious barking, accompanied by occasional pacing and a gradual decrease in her desire to engage in any form of play with Chula. By mid-January, she often refuses to go very far on her walks. Sometimes she makes it just beyond the short road leading out of our cul-de-sac and simply stops. No amount of encouragement can make her take another step forward, so I turn around, bring both dogs back home, and then go back out to walk Chula by herself.

Is it the winter cold causing Chispa's joints to stiffen up again, or is it something else? It's impossible to know for sure, but my instinct tells me it's the latter. The tension in my back and shoulders returns, the constant throbbing a physical metaphor for my aching heart and soul. I need a quiet space, both literally and figuratively, in which to center myself, to prepare myself for whatever lies ahead. I find myself longing for the Dog Chapel, for the way in which what is both within it and upon its walls opens my heart and fills me with a deep sense of peace and strength.

THREE DAYS LATER, we're on our way to Littleton for the weekend. Marisel drives and I sit in the back seat with the dogs. Chispa, now an anxious rider, whines until she becomes tired and falls asleep. Chula's nervous in the car, too. She shakes and pants and looks as if she might vomit up her entire breakfast and then some at any moment. I sit between the dogs with a towel draped across my knees, ready for all contingencies.

It's early in the morning, and even with the car's heat set as high as it will go I feel cold. The dogs are bundled up in their fleece-lined winter coats, and I'm glad for the warmth of their bodies beside me. As we drive north along the parkway through Franconia Notch, Marisel and I each place the back of a bare hand against the car window. It's a silly little ritual we've performed for years, ever since we first began coming to Littleton together. The temperature in the Notch is always about ten degrees colder than anywhere else, and the bare hand test is our best indicator of how cold we can expect to be twenty-plus miles north of the Notch. Marisel beats me to the window by about two tenths of a second.

"Oh my God, feel the glass."

"I know—it's freezing."

"I'd say it's probably about . . . what—five degrees?"

I figure the wind chill factor into that, add ten degrees, subtract a few more for the additional twelve miles north we'll travel from Littleton to St. Johnsbury, and feel that slight sense of panic I always experience when I think about being cold.

"Do you think we'll be warm enough in the chapel?"

"Don't worry, Pea, we'll be fine."

She looks at me through the rear view mirror and smiles.

I smile back, then turn away to gaze out the window. Almost immediately, I forget about the temperature. Even after all the years of traveling back and forth on this particular stretch of highway, driving through Franconia Notch still makes me catch my breath. The highway becomes one lane here as it winds through the craggy, gray granite cliffs of the Notch, rising dramatically on either side of the road. The lovely Profile Lake is stark and lonely, and there's no one walking along the sandy beach on the north end of the deep blue, numbing waters of Echo Lake. They're all missing it, I think—missing the perfect, crystalline beauty of this moment. I feel fortunate to be driving along this gorgeous stretch of road at this precise moment, blessed to be among the ones not missing it.

The following morning, while many of our neighbors in the North Country are in church, Marisel, the dogs, and I are on our way to the Dog Chapel. We pull into the empty parking lot, get out of the Jeep, and walk across the lawn to the chapel. We settle ourselves into a pew, the shine and feel of the wood both familiar and comforting to me. The Native American flute music has a calming effect on Chispa. Her whining quiets and she lies still on the floor beside Marisel.

I realize I'm not quite ready to sit, and get back up to walk around the sanctuary with Chula and read some of the notes on the walls. It's uncanny, the way I always seem to find what my heart needs among the layers of words left behind by others. I wish it were this simple in my church back in Cambridge, where I often sit and listen to words that, though crafted into the kind of intellectual and liberal-minded sermons that should resonate with me, require much reinvention and revision on my part in order to create any relevant meaning from them. Perhaps it has to do with the contrast between words meant to be processed by the brain and words meant to be consumed by the heart. Regardless, I find myself having to work hard for spiritual sustenance in church, but never here in the Dog Chapel.

On this day, what I find to nourish my soul are prayers. They're nothing like those found in the Book of Common Prayer, yet I find them every bit as affecting, in both wording and intent.

> "Kodiak—I pray you are one with all the peace, beauty, and joy you deserve. We love you."

> "Jake—You were my light and shining armor! I loved you from the moment you came into my life. More than a best friend, you were my angel in doggy form. Please run free always, not to suffer in pain or adversity. Always remember what a good dog you were. My heart goes on . . . but I miss you . . ."

"Your patch of white on your chest always spoke
to me of your loyalty, your goodness, and purity
of heart and spirit. Bear, I have loved being your
guardian and friend . . . wherever you are, please
know I will always love you forever and ever, and
ever, amen."

And then there's this.

"Heavenly Father, who knows and cares for all
creatures. I ask your blessing on my dear companion
Toby, who is very ill. Please make him well and
strong again to return to the center of our family
life. He is a good and gentle soul, who relishes life
to the fullest and enhances mine. Grant him the
gift of more fruitful years to enjoy this beautiful
world."

To which I whisper, "Amen."

As I stare at Toby's picture, I hope that everything his
person prayed for on his behalf has come to pass. The prayer
is so beautiful, so heartfelt, and says nearly everything I want
to say on behalf of my own dogs, only better. So why not just
use it?

I remove the prayer for Toby from the wall, walk back to
the pew with Chula, and sit down next to Marisel. Chispa
has fallen into a deep sleep, and I lean over Marisel for a few
seconds to watch the soft rise and fall of Chispa's rib cage, the
gentle and rhythmic movement that confirms she's still alive,
that there's still a reason for prayer.

Marisel glances over at the piece of paper in my hand.

"What's that?"

"A little prayer I took from the wall."

She looks at me with a strange expression.

"I'm going to put it back. I just want to use it to pray for
Chispa and Chula."

"What about praying for us?"

"Not with this prayer. This one's just for dogs. But I'll say a prayer for us when I'm done. And you should, too."

"I know. I will."

I lean over and kiss her cheek. Prayer isn't her thing, so this is a big concession. It's getting very cold in the Dog Chapel, and I want to say my prayers and leave while I can still feel my toes. I begin.

"Heavenly Father, who knows and cares for all creatures. I ask your blessing on my dear companion Chispa, who is very ill. Please make her well and strong again, to return to the center of our family life. She is a good and gentle soul, who relishes life to the fullest and enriches mine. Grant her the gift of more fruitful years to enjoy this beautiful world. May all these things be so. Amen."

I repeat the prayer for Chula, modifying it slightly to account for the fact that she's injured, not ill, and then sit in silence, my heart open to God's response.

After some moments of silence, I glance over at Marisel.

"Sweetie, let's say a prayer for us and then let's go. It's freezing in here."

"Okay, Pea."

I close my eyes, take a few slow deep breaths, and wait for the right words to come to me. Words and phrases ricochet back and forth across my mind, a word here, a fragment or sentence there, until they all fall into place, creating a fully formed, silent prayer.

Dear God, may all those I love but see no longer, both animal and human, keep me and Marisel in their loving sight and care. May their love weave itself around us and hold us together in the difficult days ahead as we struggle to make sense of illness and grief. May they help us reach out to one another in love and kindness, instead of turning away in anger and frustration, and may their wisdom guide us toward an understanding of how to be compassionate caregivers. And when the time comes to let Chispa go, may we do so gracefully, unselfishly, and with much gratitude for the gift of life that must now be relinquished. And through it all, may Marisel and I be a source of support and comfort for each other and never lose sight of the belief that at its core, life is about love and joy and hope. May all these things be so. Amen.

This is the prayer I send out into the Dog Chapel. Not too long-winded, but substantial enough, I hope, to catch God's attention. I don't know what Marisel's prayer is, or if she's even praying at all. Whether she is or isn't doesn't really matter, I tell myself. God is either listening or not, and if not, one more prayer isn't going to make any difference. I open my eyes and glance over at Marisel. She sits quietly, eyes closed. Maybe she is praying after all.

She feels me staring at her and opens her eyes.

"Are you ready to go, Pea?"

"Are you?"

"Yup."

She leans over and gently shakes Chispa awake, and I walk with Chula back over to the wall where I'd removed the prayer for Toby. I replace it, my hand lingering on the piece of paper. Be well, sweet boy.

"Okay, Chula-bula, let's go."

We catch up with Marisel and Chispa waiting for us near the door, and as we follow them down the steps I glance behind me one more time. I always find it so hard to leave the Dog Chapel.

SIX

IN THE WEEKS following our visit to the Dog Chapel Chispa's behavior turns a corner, and not in the direction I've prayed for. Her barking increases to the point of near intolerability and brings my noise sensitivity to the edge of its breaking point. She paces aimlessly around the house, always counterclockwise—living room, dining room, kitchen—as if she's forgotten where her bed or the chaise she usually sleeps on are. She tries to bite people she's known most of her life, and her eyes more often than not have a vacant look in them, that same look I've noticed off and on for over a year. She's been house trained ever since she's lived with us, but now she's having accidents.

As the aggregate of these behaviors finally cuts through the fog of denial that's been obscuring all rational vision, I am, at long last, willing to take the step Bari's been suggesting for quite some time now. I make an appointment for Chispa to be seen by Dr. Andrew Farabaugh, a neurologist at Angell Animal Medical Center in Jamaica Plain. Angell is one of the best animal hospitals in the country, and I feel fortunate to have access to it.

Dr. Farabaugh takes a detailed history of Chispa's symptoms—length, progression, severity—and asks about the medications she takes, how effective they've been at controlling symptoms, any noticeable or notable side effects—the works. I marvel at his thoroughness. I can't remember the last time a doctor took my own medical history with such precision and in such depth.

He watches Chispa walk, tests her reflexes, palpates her spine for cervical pain. Everything appears normal, except for a bit of bilateral pelvic limb lameness. He jots down a few notes and then turns to me.

"How's her appetite?"

"Great. That's probably the only thing that hasn't changed."

"Does she sleep through the night?"

"Yes."

I don't give him the longer version of my answer to this question. I can't bring myself to tell him that the blessedly quiet night-time hours are a God-send, the only time I can find peace, the only time I feel like a fully integrated human being in my own home.

Dr. Farabaugh is so kind and patient, with both Chispa and me. Chispa barks and paces throughout the entirety of her hour-long appointment, but Dr. Farabaugh never once raises his voice over the noise or shows the least bit of frustration with her. He simply points out what he's observing and acknowledges how difficult it must be to live with the constant vocalizing.

I'm grateful for his understanding. But his patience, in such stark contrast with my own increasing lack thereof, makes me feel deeply ashamed of myself. I watch now as Chispa paces back and forth in the exam room, her loud, anxious barking bouncing off the walls and echoing in my head. She's my dog, and I love her with my whole heart. Why, then, do I find it so difficult to be patient with her lately, so easy to raise my voice in frustration? She deserves better. My throat tightens, and I dig the nail of my middle finger sharply into the tender area beneath the thumb. The sound of Dr. Farabaugh's voice interrupts my thoughts, providing the welcome relief of turning my attention elsewhere.

"Well, I think I have some answers for you as to what's been going on with Chispa."

Something in the tone of his voice, the expression in his eyes, gives away the fact that there's no happy ending here. My sense of relief vanishes. Instead, a profound dread rushes through my blood, turning my skin clammy and my insides cold. The room seems smaller, the air less plentiful. I'm terrified to hear whatever it is he's about to tell me. God, please let his beeper go off, I pray. Please let him leave this room and never return to tell me exactly what's wrong with my dog.

But he stays.

"I believe the anxiety you've been noticing over the past year and a half or so really hasn't been separation anxiety, but a symptom of dementia. Based on everything I've been able to determine through her examination, I think she's suffering from something called canine cognitive dysfunction."

I already know the answer to the question I'm about to ask, learned it no more than ten seconds ago. But because I can't think of anything else to say, I ask it anyway.

"Is that a form of dementia?"

"Yes, it is."

I'd always considered dementia to be an illness of the mind. What I didn't understand, not for a long time, is that it's also a disease of the body. It wasn't until several years ago, when Marisel's father Tomas was dying from what she and I believed was congestive heart failure but was actually a combination of congestive heart failure and advanced dementia, that I learned the truth about the disease during an emotional phone conversation with his doctor: dementia is considered a terminal illness. While the symptoms of early-stage dementia are primarily cognitive, as the disease progresses the brain not only forgets where things belong or who people are, it forgets to instruct the heart to pump blood and the lungs to inhale oxygen. It had never occurred to me to connect the cognitive and the somatic in this way, but once the connection was made the entire horrifying arc of the disease became clear.

And so, when Dr. Farabaugh confirms that canine cognitive dysfunction is a form of dementia, I understand that, one way or another, the diagnosis is a death sentence for Chispa. But giving up on her is inconceivable. I ask him if there's something we can do, some other medication we can try.

He tells me about a new medication called Anipryl. Several recent studies on the use of Anipryl for canine cognitive dysfunction have shown promising results, and he knows of a few vets who've used it with some success. This is pretty much all that remains to be tried, he tells me. As he writes out the prescription for Anipryl, something else occurs to him. He says we might also consider using another drug along with the Anipryl, a drug called Nicergoline. It's been approved in Europe for treating age-related behavioral disorders in dogs, and might increase Anipryl's effectiveness.

In the end we agree to start out with the Anipryl and see how that goes. If it's not effective, we'll add the Nicergoline.

"And what if neither of these works? Is there anything else we can try?"

When he answers, the sadness in his voice nearly breaks me. No, he tells me. If these medications don't work, there's nothing more to be done.

SEVEN

IN THE HALF hour it takes to drive home from Angell, I inexplicably begin to doubt everything Dr. Farabaugh has just told me, everything I believed made perfect sense just ten minutes earlier. I tell myself he can't know anything definitive without a brain scan, without tests of some kind. He didn't see her brain, I reason, so how can he really know? I glance through the rear-view mirror into the back seat, where Chispa, exhausted from her ordeal, is in a deep sleep. Does she understand what's happening to her? Is she bothered by it? I have no way of knowing.

When I get home I Google "canine cognitive dysfunction" and find a surprising number of links. I wonder how many dogs are afflicted with this disease. Are the percentages comparable to Alzheimer's in the human population? It doesn't really matter; this isn't the information I'm looking for. What I'm looking for is proof. I want to see Chispa's exact set of symptoms laid out in one of these Google entries. I need to be convinced that Dr. Farabaugh, without benefit of tests or scans, has made the correct diagnosis.

I click on the link that appears at the top of the search and begin reading. I learn that the full name of the disease is Canine Cognitive Dysfunction Syndrome, or CDS. I scan the list of symptoms—dogs with CDS are confused, distant, lost or withdrawn, unwilling to play, don't recognize and are startled by family members, pace, tremble when lying down, sleep more during the day and less at night, frequently soil in the house, stare at walls or into space, and seek less time, attention, and play from their family members.

I return to the top of the list and begin a slow and thorough examination of each symptom. I'm looking for the ones that don't fit, the ones that will prove Dr. Farabaugh wrong. But the symptoms at the top of the list seem right on target—Chispa is confused, distant, and seems lost and withdrawn. Not always, but often enough to count these symptoms as applicable. It's true that she sometimes doesn't recognize me or Marisel, and the last time my parents came to visit she tried to bite my mother. Is she startled by us? I don't know. She jumps when I touch her if she's been asleep, but who doesn't startle when they're suddenly awakened? I mentally cross that symptom off the list.

Pacing? Yes. Trembling while lying down? Yes, though she's done this for many, many years. Is it worse now? Maybe, but I can't say for sure. Since the answer doesn't present as a definitive yes, I decide this symptom is simply part of Chispa's personality and discard it. Does she sleep more during the day than during the night? No—she sleeps somewhere in the area of twenty-one hours a day, and sleeps through the night. Frequent soiling in the house . . . I ask myself how "frequent" is defined in this context. Once a day, every other day, multiple times a day? Or, for a dog who was completely house-trained from the day we got her, does "at all" qualify for counting this symptom? I decide that it doesn't, but that several times a week does.

Stares at the walls or into space. She doesn't stare at the walls, but she does stare into space. Often. This symptom counts. And it's true that she seeks less attention from us, doesn't want to play anymore. She doesn't want to go on her walks anymore either, though this could be attributed to her aching joints. Even allowing for that possibility, though, I think this symptom also counts.

I make a mental tally of the symptoms that apply to Chispa, and admit to myself that the diagnosis of CDS seems a good fit. Incredibly, though, I'm still not convinced. It's not that I doubt the diagnosis based on the symptoms listed. My doubt comes from the one symptom noticeably absent from the list, the symptom that, for Chispa, is the most obvious and pronounced: loud and incessant vocalizing. If that's not listed as a primary symptom, I rationalize, then she can't possibly have CDS. It has to be something else.

I scan further down the page, looking for a mention of vocalization. What I find is something else entirely, something that brings me up close and personal with reality. It's a piece of information I already possess, but seeing the words written out lends a weight to them, a weight absent from the spoken word.

The words I read on the computer screen represent a truth I both know and deny: "There is no cure for CDS."

I stare at these words for a while, as if I expect them to transform into something else under my intense scrutiny, something more palatable, more hopeful. I begin to reconsider the wisdom of trying one more medication. What's the point of helping my beloved dog live longer with this terrible disease that there's no cure for? But almost immediately after my mind forms this thought, I retreat to my fallback position of doubt and questioning. What if Chispa doesn't really have CDS? Where's the mention of the vocalizing? Dr. Farabaugh must have been wrong. It must be something else, something that can be cured.

I close the page and open another. Here I learn that the cause of CDS is unknown, but autopsies on dogs suffering from the disease have shown degenerative brain lesions similar to those found in Alzheimer's patients. The author has grouped CDS symptoms into a catchy little acronym: DISH. Disorientation, Interaction changes, Sleep changes, House soiling. Oddly, the image I see when I read the acronym is of Chispa, standing in front of her dog dish, consuming her food with her usual gusto.

There's nothing new, so I click on another link. I read more about autopsies, and learn that amyloid plaque, which affects certain areas of cognition, has been discovered in the brains of both CDS dogs and Alzheimer's patients. And then, finally, I come across the words I'm both looking for and hoping never to find: "easily agitated and barks for no reason." There's more—vocalizing, panting, and restlessness, no longer greeting family members or caring about being petted. It all fits together now, into a nearly textbook and heartbreaking diagnosis. My formerly playful and loving dog, once so engaged with the world around her, has Canine Cognitive Dysfunction Syndrome. The sorrow I feel at this realization numbs me beyond tears.

I stare out the window of my second-floor study for a long time, at the empty cul-de-sac below. This is Chispa's neighborhood, the streets and sidewalks a never-ending source of smells and squirrels, of long, exploratory escorted walks. I see an image of myself walking with Chispa and Laika down the middle of the street in the usually quiet cul-de-sac, our backs heading away from the house. It's an odd sensation, seeing us like this—as if I'm detached from my own life in some fundamental way, an outsider spying on myself.

In this vision of us I'm wearing my red LL Bean barn jacket, so it must be fall, though the leaves are still green. Early fall, then. Chispa and Laika walk out ahead of me on the tandem leash, tails wagging, Chispa's with that funny whirligig pattern that appeared when she was four, right after she recovered from her stroke. I can't see our faces but I'm certain we're smiling, they in anticipation of an adventure, I with the contentment of being in their company. As we round the bend out of the cul-de-sac, headed toward the more interesting (from a dog's perspective) Doonan Street, life is good. I've never heard of Canine Cognitive Dysfunction Syndrome, and in the blissful ignorance and simple joy of that moment, it's impossible to imagine the future that's become the present.

But that unimaginable future stares back at me now from the computer screen, clarifying the recent past, defining the present, and providing a window into what's to come. I'm suddenly overwhelmed by a feeling of utter helplessness that evolves into an oddly hollow mixture of anger and profound sadness. Why my dog? Isn't abandonment on a beach, a stroke, thyroid disease, and arthritis suffering enough for one canine lifetime?

Apparently not.

Wallowing isn't something I find useful or attractive. But I immerse myself in it now, wallowing in the bitterness I feel toward whatever unseen forces have conspired to allow Chispa to end her life in this manner. It's not fair. I repeat these words over and over again, like a mantra: "It's not fair."

Maybe it's this repetition of truth to whatever power that brings about the mental shift. Suddenly I'm energized, ready to take on CDS. I type "Anipryl" into Google. On each web page I open, there are testimonials from people whose dogs have been completely changed by the drug. These dogs no longer pace or vocalize, have regained their interest in the world around them, recognize and seek attention from the people they love. There are some stories that aren't as positive, some dogs for whom the medication doesn't work, but these stories don't stick, don't hold any credence. Instead, I choose to believe that Anipryl is the miracle drug I've been praying for.

I discuss the results of my research with Marisel, and we decide to get the Anipryl prescription filled. Chispa needs to be off Prozac for two weeks before she can begin taking Anipryl, and we begin the process of weaning her off it immediately. As the end of the two Prozac-free weeks finally approaches, I drive over to Angell to pick up the Anipryl. It's ridiculously expensive but I don't care. I'd pay anything for the chance at a normal life for Chispa.

In the car, I open the bag and take out the box of Anipryl. I look at it again. It's just a package of pills, like so many others I've picked up for my animals over the years. But though its outside appearance is unremarkable, what's inside the box is anything but. Sealed within each individual bubble is the miracle, the magic bullet—the pill that will restore Chispa to herself and to me. As I drive out of the parking lot onto Huntington Avenue, I remember what Dr. Farabaugh told me: up to eighty percent of dogs treated with Anipryl show some improvement after being treated for longer than a month. Those seem like excellent odds to me.

In retrospect, I realize that when considering Dr. Farabaugh's words, I paid no attention to what were perhaps the two most important ones. They were small words, the kind that have a tendency to dissipate in the space between being spoken and being understood, but together they formed a significant phrase—"up to." I'm sure these words seemed nothing more than unnecessary fillers to me at the time, if I noticed them at all.

And so I give Chispa her first dose of Anipryl with stratospherically high hopes, and wait for the miracle.

EIGHT

A MONTH LATER the results of the medication are clear, and so is the meaning of those tiny words I glossed over. "Up to" does not mean a definitive eighty percent—it means that eighty percent is the maximum percentage possible. This fact obviously lowers the odds of success, though it's impossible to know to what extent. But whatever the actual odds, Chispa doesn't beat them—she's in the percentage of dogs for whom the medication doesn't work.

I'm devastated.

I call Dr. Farabaugh to ask about bolstering the Anipryl with Nicergoline, but ultimately decide against this option. Anipryl was so completely ineffective for Chispa's particular configuration of CDS that adding a booster drug isn't likely to produce any significant improvement. I don't ask him the other question on my mind, though, the question I've been obsessing about since the Anipryl failure: Did my decision to go the non-pharmaceutical route back when all this first began have anything to do with the drug's inability to help Chispa? Did I let things go too far, beyond the point where a drug like Anipryl could be effective?

I don't ask because I'm terrified of the answer. Although hearing that my decision had nothing to do with anything would be an enormous relief, I don't feel strong enough to risk the damage to my psyche that would result from hearing that it possibly did. Instead, I think back to Chispa's appointment with Dr. Farabaugh, remember the last thing he said to me. *If these medications don't work, there's nothing more to be done.* Nothing except pray.

DURING THE DRIVE from Littleton to St. Johnsbury, I
sit in the back seat with Chispa, holding her against me, trying
to ease her anxiety.

"It's okay . . . you're okay."

I run my hand down her head and along her side, speaking
the same words over and over, as if the act of repetition will
somehow transform them into truth. Her anxious whining
continues.

I hope we'll have some time alone in the Dog Chapel. I
want to be able to sit quietly in a pew, with Marisel and Chispa
beside me, and pray. There's no point in praying for Chispa's
recovery; I know enough about dementia to understand that.
But I want her to have a sense of calm, to be able to exist
within her physical being with minimal anxiety. I want there
to be things in her ever narrowing world that make her joyful,
the way going for her morning walk or lying in the sun on the
asphalt used to. I want whatever time she has left with us to be
as easy for her as possible, and I hope that whatever manifesta-
tion of the divine I've felt so many times in the Dog Chapel
will hear my prayers for the dog I love so much. I'm not
asking for a miracle. Not anymore. All I'm asking for is a small
amount of peace and happiness for Chispa. How difficult can
that be to conjure up if you're the Almighty?

When we arrive at the Dog Chapel I'm relieved to find the
parking area empty, but the irony of the moment doesn't
escape me. In earlier times, my relief at seeing an empty parking lot would have been directly related to not having to deal
with the possibility of encountering other dogs. But I no
longer worry about that. There are two positive changes that
have resulted from Chispa's dementia—she's not aggressive
toward other dogs anymore, mostly because she doesn't notice
them, and she doesn't seem to remember that thunderstorms
and fireworks terrify her. Other than these two blessings,
neither of which is small, there's nothing to recommend
Chispa's current state of mind.

We get out of the car and begin the trek across the lawn to the chapel, our treaded boots crunching the packed-down snow with every step. The sound is a memory trigger, and fragments of other winter scenes suddenly appear, unbidden, in my mind's eye.

I see Chispa trotting briskly through our yard in the freshly fallen snow, tail wagging and nose to the ground, snorting and blowing little spurts of white as she carves a zigzag pattern in the snow with her nose. I see her standing on the back porch waiting to be let in from having done her business, her red coat covered with snowflakes. I see her wearing the same red coat, standing beside Laika in our driveway in Littleton, right next to Marisel's Jeep. On top of the Jeep, our freshly cut Christmas tree is secured to the roof rack by a rope tied into a series of elaborate loops and knots. There's a light snowfall, and the picture Marisel snaps of that moment becomes our holiday card that year.

But the snow that once energized and stimulated Chispa means nothing to her now. It's just something that falls on the ground and on her body, something to walk through in order to get somewhere else. To me, though, the sight of snow-covered Dog Mountain on this morning is achingly lovely. It's the kind of beauty that, in its utter perfection, sometimes blends with and magnifies pain in a way that's difficult to put into words but pierces to the core, and I'm relieved when we reach the door of the Dog Chapel and walk inside.

Marisel and I don't take the time to read any of the notes on the wall today. I experience a moment of regret over this, as if not bearing witness to the lives of the dogs and people I feel I've in some virtual sense come to know is almost sacrilegious in this space. But my emotional edges feel worn, barely able to support my own grief. I'm sure those whose words and pictures surround me will understand if I visit with them another day. Today is for Chispa.

We sit in our favorite pew, the one on the left with the black Lab sides, and say nothing to each other. My eyes wander around the chapel, settling on the stained glass window with the image of a black Lab's head and face, tongue extended, as if about to greet her person in a soggy explosion of canine happiness. "Joy," the window's caption reads.

I've been contemplating this word and its meaning, its place in Chispa's life, a great deal lately. In so many ways, joy has characterized her life. And now, in an almost perverse reversal of all that has been, it's the apparent absence of joy that has come to define her life, has become the measure by which I begin to assess its quality. What is the true significance of joy in a life worth living? When I consider the words that define joy—a sense of well-being, bliss, delight, happiness, pleasure— I can't imagine a life without joy for myself.

But what is it like for Chispa? I spend hours lying awake at night, wondering how a dog experiences a life in which nearly everything that once brought joy no longer matters. Does she feel the absence of joy from her life? Does it sadden her? Or does she have no sense that something once so integral to her life is missing? Perhaps she's perfectly content with the one joy that's still accessible to her—the joy she finds in eating. I wish I knew.

Then again, I wonder if I'm anthropomorphizing, attempting to assess the quality of Chispa's life based upon what I want and need in my own. Still, when I return to the definition of joy, it seems in no way non-applicable to the life of a dog: a sense of well-being and bliss, the kind that leads to a profound contentedness and a connection to the things that delight.

My dog is clearly not content, either with herself or her surroundings. Her relationship to the people and places she once loved is no longer a source of comfort and happiness but of extreme and continual anxiety. As for connection to what delights, she's absolutely connected to the one thing that still rocks her world—food. But is this what her joy, once so expansive, has been reduced to? And is a life based on connection to nothing more than food a life worth living, even for a dog? Once again, I wish I knew—wish that, in some way that would leave no room for even the most minute fragment of uncertainty, she could tell me her truth.

I close my eyes and let the sacred flute music wash over me until I feel a sensation of being lifted, of being just that much closer to God. I open my eyes for a brief moment to glance over at Chispa, and see that she's fallen asleep. Good, I tell myself. Good.

I close my eyes again, and as I open my heart to the powerful emotions of the place, my prayer for Chispa begins to take form. It's a silent prayer, like all the others posted on the walls around me, and I release it from the confines of my mind into the space of the Dog Chapel: "Chispa, for whatever days remain, may your dog soul be joyful, as joyful as your love has made my own soul, and filled with peace. May you always know how much you're loved, and may I know when, finally, it's time to let go. Amen."

As these words take their unseen place in the Dog Chapel, I'm filled with a deep sense of calm, a belief that everything from this point forward will be as it's meant to be. I open my eyes and turn to look at Marisel. She's been watching me, waiting.

"I've said my prayer now. Are you ready to go?"

She nods and leans down to wake Chispa.

"C'mon, good girl. Let's go."

Chispa rises stiffly from the floor. She stands very still for a moment, then shakes her body. It's only a half-shake, really—nothing like the vigorous, head-to-the-very-tip-of-the-tail way she used to shake herself into full wakefulness. It's as if her body still recalls the mechanics of the action, but her mind has long since forgotten its purpose. I hook her leash to her collar, and the three of us walk from the sanctuary into the vestibule.

When we reach the chapel door, Chispa stops. We stand for a short time on the granite steps while I wait for the tug on the leash indicating she's ready to move on. She lifts her head slightly and points her nose to one side, then the other, then directly in front of us, sniffing the thin winter air that smells like snow and woods and blue sky. Watching her reminds me of the way I inhale when I think I'll never return to a place and want to commit its scent to memory. I've always wondered, when recalling this moment, if she somehow knew then what I could not yet allow myself to accept.

The Word of Dog
JOY

"Cloudy—You opened my heart to life and brought me joy every day. You are not just in my heart, you are my heart."

"Sweet Tiko—Thank you for the gift of 12 years of joy. You are the most amazing dog."

"Gulliver—The golden king of our hearts and the inspiration for so much in our lives; always a source of joy."

"To Gus and Skye—We'll remember you always! And Moses. You gave us joy."

"Abbey Lane: To say that I miss you and love you so much barely scratches the surface. For 12 years you were like my child, you brought so much joy into my life and taught me things no other human could. You even taught me how to say goodbye."

"Dear Cassidy & Barney—Buddies until the end—You lived when dogs could roam free. You both brought so much joy to all who loved you. We hope you are roaming freely, together, still. Thanks for waiting until I got on the bus every morning."

"Sugar as her name implied was a sweet dog, always with a smile on her face and a wag in her tail. She greeted everyone as a friend. She especially enjoyed the company of small children. She would engage them in social settings and wanted to be in the middle of their party no matter what they were doing . . . She loved her walks and was an avid explorer of the 'thicket' that no human dare enter . . . She was a consummate camper and loved spending long lazy hours in the tall grass of summer. Of course the food around the camp fire was another one of her favorites!"

"Dear Teacup—You made us happy every day. We sang songs to you and you would tilt your head back and forth. I like to think of you running fast in a cool park with a clear path, just the way you liked."

NINE

JOY. IRONICALLY, IT was the absence of joy that, through a series of plans made and broken and changed, brought Chispa into my life.

Over thirteen years ago I'd gone to Vieques, a small island in the Caribbean, hoping to begin the healing process after losing Comet. Learning to live without her had been challenging, a repetitive cycle of new reality learned and committed to memory and then promptly forgotten, overshadowed by the recollections of our life together that poked through the cracks in my heart like tiny flowers straining to reach the sunlight. Even a modicum of peace had been elusive.

Still, I thought that healing, if it came at all, might come from the soul-soothing combination of warm sun, sea, and trade winds. Instead, it came in a more unexpected form—that of an abandoned dog on the long crescent of sparsely populated Sun Bay Beach: a dog whose physical makeup reminded me so much of Comet that my chest tightened at the sight of her and I found myself wanting to run both toward and away from her; a dog who settled herself beside our beach chairs for the afternoon and raced after us as we drove away, keeping up until I happened to glance in the side-view mirror and see her blurred body in a cloud of dust, keeping up until we stopped for her.

IT'S BEEN TWO and a half months since Comet died, and the deep and constant missing of her has yet to subside. Perhaps it never will. Marisel and I are going to Disney World in a few weeks, the trip her idea. She loves Disney World, and hopes that time spent in a place of magical fantasy might jump-start the process of moving through and out of my grief. She talks about our upcoming vacation daily, and I feign enthusiasm. I don't really want to go to Disney World.

But it's more than simply not wanting to go. It's an unshakeable feeling that I *can't* go—the feeling that if I do, something in the universe will become badly and forever misaligned. And so, finally, as we sit at the kitchen table one morning drinking our coffee, I tell Marisel I don't want to go.

"Why?"

I have no logical or adequate answer to this question, so I say nothing.

"I thought you were excited about going . . ."

"I wasn't . . . not really. I just wanted to go somewhere, anywhere that isn't here and doesn't remind me of losing Comet. I'm sorry . . ."

"It's okay. We still have time to cancel our reservation."

I hear the disappointment in her voice, know how excited she'd been about going. We need another plan.

"Can we go somewhere else?" I ask.

"If you want to. It's kind of last minute, so I'm not sure what our options would be. Where do you want to go?"

"I don't know . . . Maybe one of the islands, one we've never been to. Let's talk about it tonight when we get home."

"Okay."

The conversation has expended every bit of my limited energy, and leaves me feeling both exhausted and oddly light, as if relieved of the burden of supporting an invisible, unbearable weight. We're not going to Disney World, and I have the strange and inexplicable sense that with that decision, life has somehow started over.

OUR ISSUE OF *Caribbean Life and Travel* arrives that day, and I scoop it up from the table in the foyer along with the rest of the mail when I return home from work. Laika, now our only dog, rushes over to greet me, skidding across the hardwood floors in her excitement. I reach down to pet her head, wondering if she has any idea how dependent I've become on her since Comet died. I hope not, because I think it would stress her out to know. She's not cut out for the alpha dog role. She's too sensitive, too shy.

It's a warm spring day, and I take her outside to sit on the back porch with me while I browse through the magazine. I randomly thumb through the pages until something catches my attention—an article about Vieques, an off-island of Puerto Rico. I read the article with interest, my excitement growing as I take in the beauty of the accompanying photographs—the stunning and nearly deserted beaches, the historic fort and lighthouse, the wild horses clustered beneath the palm trees on a beach called Sun Bay.

Something tells me this is it, this is where we're supposed to go. When Marisel comes home I show her the article, and she agrees—this is the place. It's beautiful, we've never been there, neither have most other people, and it's affordable. Marisel books everything—villa, flight to Puerto Rico, flight to Vieques—the next day.

GETTING TO VIEQUES is an all-day affair. We leave Boston at seven o'clock in the morning and don't arrive at the rented villa until late that afternoon. The house sits on a bluff overlooking the ocean, and the muffled sound of waves breaking below works magic on our travel-frayed nerves. We finish unpacking, go out for dinner, and spend the rest of the evening planning our first full day on the island.

Vieques is, at the time, an island with a significant and controversial U.S. military presence. The military regularly conducts maneuvers and exercises on some of the island's most beautiful, out of the way beaches, and anyone planning a trip to one of these "color" beaches—Red, Blue, Green—has to call the morning of to confirm that the beach is cleared for civilian use. After a very long day of travel, the thought of making that call the next morning is unappealing.

"Why don't we just go to Sun Bay Beach," Marisel suggests.

I'm nervous at the prospect. Although the beach has the wild horses going for it, there's also been a rash of petty theft there over the last few months. I don't consider getting mugged on Sun Bay Beach the ideal way to kick off our vacation, but Marisel is unconcerned.

"Don't worry. I'll bring my Swiss Army knife with me, just in case."

Still not entirely convinced, I nevertheless agree to go. When we arrive at Sun Bay Beach the next morning my anxiety evaporates. As we drive along the narrow dirt road that runs parallel to the beach, I have a clear view of Sun Bay. The bay itself is breathtaking, a long expanse of turquoise water. Palm and sea grape trees grow all along the upper edges of the crescent-shaped beach, providing shade for people and horses, and the sand separating trees from water is blindingly white.

Although the beach is one of the island's most frequently visited, on this morning there aren't a lot of people—just enough to make me feel safe. We continue down the road until we come to an area of the beach that's quiet but not deserted, then pull off onto the shoulder and park our rental Jeep between a couple of palm trees, both of us looking forward to settling in for the day.

Not long after we've finished arranging our beach chairs, a small group passes by—three men and their dog. The dog reminds me of Comet . . . same slender curved tail, same racing-dog body type, same long ears sticking straight up. The familiar ache of missing her catches in my throat, tightens around my heart. The men and the dog continue down the beach, eventually becoming nothing more than four black specks in the distance. I pick up my book in an effort to forget.

I'm lost in the pages when Marisel announces she wants to move to the opposite end of the beach. I'm content where we are, but she's insistent.

"Why do you want to move to that end of the beach?" I ask. "What's the matter with where we are?"

"The water's bluer over there. I can see it through my binoculars."

"The water's bluer?"

"Yeah—much bluer."

"It looks exactly the same to me."

"Well, it's not. It's definitely bluer over there. And it looks sunnier, too."

Sunnier? The eruption of the volcano on Montserrat not too long ago has sent volcanic ash clouds drifting up the Caribbean island chain, veiling the sun in a perpetual gray haze. It's not sunnier anywhere. Still, I can see that arguing with Marisel is pointless.

"Alright, fine. Let's go."

Although I've agreed to move, I'm annoyed with her for yanking me out of my fictional world, a world in which Comet doesn't exist and never has. I let Marisel pack up most of our belongings and move them to the Jeep.

"I hope this is where you want to be, because I'm not moving again," I tell her once we've set up for the second time.

"No, this is perfect."

We settle into our beach chairs, and I return to my book. After a while the tropical heat changes from pleasant to unbearable, and we dash down to the water for a swim. Cooled off and happy, we head back to our chairs, and that's when we notice them, sitting no more than thirty feet from us—the three men and the dog. The dog that reminds me of Comet.

I immediately regret what I said about not moving again. I can't see the dog's face, have only a rear view. But everything about her is so evocative of Comet. Right on cue, the painful lump in my throat emerges, as familiar a part of me now as my left hand.

I want to look away but can't. I watch, mesmerized, as the three men walk down to the water and wade in. The dog does not accompany them into the water. She stays along the shoreline, unresponsive to their attempts to coax her in, more interested in a young man walking in her direction. She leaves the three men in the water and races up to the young man, circles around him, sniffs his leg. He reaches down to pet her but continues walking.

The men in the water call the dog again, but she refuses to join them. She sees a new group of people headed up the beach in our direction, and I watch her approach them, repeating the same behaviors as with the young man—circle, sniff, prance. They ignore her and keep walking. It's not until she can no longer see anyone on the beach that she joins the three men in the water.

Marisel has been watching the dog, too.

"That dog reminds me so much of Comet," she says.

"I know . . . it's really getting to me."

"I'm going to go talk to those guys—I want to find out what kind of dog that is."

Perhaps we'll now be one step closer to solving the mystery, to finally being able to answer the question most people asked when they saw Comet: "What kind of dog is that?"

The three men and the dog are emerging from the water, and Marisel gets up from her chair and walks over to meet them. I watch them talking, one of the men gesturing animatedly, pointing at the beach in the direction of where we'd originally been sitting. Marisel looks over at the dog, then back at the man. They chat for a few minutes more and she heads back up the sand.

"She's not their dog."

"She's not? But they walked pretty much all the way up the beach with her . . . and she seems so attached to them, doesn't she?"

"I know—but she's not theirs. Those guys are all from Italy; the one I was talking with told me the dog came out of the woods near the bath house and started walking along beside them, so they gave her some food and she stayed with them."

I glance over at the men, see that they're getting ready to pack up. The dog realizes this, too, and sits attentively beside one of their beach chairs. I hope they'll take her with them.

"He said they think she's lost," Marisel continues. "He asked if I'd noticed the way she keeps running up to everyone she sees on the beach and sniffing them, like she's looking for someone."

It's then I remember reading something I'd pushed from consciousness—a story about the dogs in Puerto Rico and the off-islands, dogs referred to as satos, dumped with regularity and indifference on island streets and beaches.

"Maybe she was abandoned," I suggest.

"But she has a collar, she must belong to someone. I think the Italian guys are right—she's lost."

Lost is much more palatable to me than abandoned.

"Yeah, you're probably right . . ."

But what if she's not right? What then?

As the men begin packing up their belongings the dog becomes anxious. She sees one of the men pick up the white Styrofoam cooler and trudge over toward the car, and she trots off after him. Another of the men passes by her on his way to the car, lugging towels and several large, rolled-up straw beach mats. The dog becomes more agitated, looking frantically from one man to the next. She notices Marisel and me sitting calmly in our beach chairs just a short distance away and runs toward us, then plops herself onto the sand next to Marisel.

The man Marisel spoke with earlier passes by, carrying the group's remaining belongings to the car. He looks over at us and waves.

"Ciao."

He stops for a moment and smiles at me, gesturing at the dog with his head.

"Nice dog. Maybe you can take her home with you, no?"

I smile back at him. "Maybe."

The dog remains with us for the rest of the afternoon, and when we begin to gather up our things she walks over to the Jeep and sits down beside the passenger door. Marisel and I look at each other.

"What are we going to do?" I ask.

"We can't take her with us, Pea."

"Why not?"

"Because she has a collar on. She belongs to someone."

"But if she's lost, don't you think we should take her with us and try to find out where she belongs?"

"I guess so . . . Let's drive her down to the bath house. Maybe she belongs to the man we saw working there when we drove in, or maybe he knows whose dog she is."

I open the door and pull the passenger seat forward. The dog hops in and settles herself in the back seat. Marisel tosses our beach gear into the small trunk space and we drive back down the narrow dirt road to the bath house near the beach entrance. As we approach the white cement building, we see the same man who was there earlier in the day. He's still hard at work, trimming bushes with a battered pair of garden shears. Marisel pulls up in front of the building and we both get out to speak with the man. Before I have a chance to close the door behind me, the dog jumps out and follows along.

Marisel points to the dog, asking the man if she belongs to him.

"No, *no es mío.*"

Dogs aren't allowed on the beach, he explains. He wants to make sure we understand he's not breaking any rules, and once reassured suggests she may belong to someone in the village.

"How far is the village from here?" I ask.

The man looks at Marisel, waiting for her translation.

"Ah. *No está muy lejos—dos milas de aqui, más o menos, a la derecha.*"

A couple of miles up the road, on the right. Simple enough.

The dog is busily sniffing at something around the base of a palm tree, completely absorbed in whatever scent she's discovered. She seems oblivious to our presence, and the man turns to us, suggests that this would be a good time to leave. He is sure she'll find her way home. I'm not nearly as sure, but Marisel and I get back in the Jeep anyway.

As we pull away and begin driving toward the beach's exit, I happen to glance in the side-view mirror. The dog is chasing after us, her dark body blurred by her speed and the cloud of dust the Jeep's tires kick up in the soft dirt. I can't bear the sight of it.

"That's it—stop the car! We're not leaving her behind in the dust."

Marisel stops the Jeep and I get out. I hold the door open for the dog, and as she catches up with us, panting, her eyes meet mine. Then she leaps into the back and collapses onto the seat in an exhausted heap.

We spend what remains of the afternoon driving around the area, trying to find the dog's home. We start with the tiny village the groundskeeper mentioned, ask everyone we see if they recognize the dog. No one does. We drive to another, slightly larger village in the opposite direction. Nobody there recognizes her either, although one woman tells us she thinks the dog may belong to a woman who works at a local inn. So we drive to the inn, where the woman agrees that the dog certainly looks like her dog. She pokes her head through the car window for a closer look, then confirms the dog isn't hers. Not knowing where else to look, we give up and head back to our villa, stopping at a nearby supermarket to buy some dog food and flea shampoo.

THE NEXT DAY, we exhaust all efforts to locate the dog's people. Marisel calls the police station, asks if anyone has reported a lost dog. Negative. I call the local animal shelter and speak with a woman named Stephanie.

"Has anyone called there looking for their dog?"

"No, I'm afraid not . . . Did you find a dog somewhere?"

"Yes, on Sun Bay Beach."

"Oh. Unfortunately, I'm sure the dog was dumped there. It happens all the time."

"But she's wearing a collar, so she must belong to someone, right?"

"Probably not . . . We see a lot of dogs dumped still wearing their collars. Where's the dog now?"

"With me, in our villa. But we're only going to be here for the week."

Stephanie pauses before speaking again. "It'd be really great for the dog if you took her home with you . . . Do you think you might consider it?"

I look over at the dog. She's lying quietly on the cool tile floor, front legs outstretched, chin resting on crossed paws, watching me. We make eye contact and her tail wags wildly, brushing across the floor, the sound of it just audible. I know right then that there's no way I'm leaving Vieques without her. This dog is the reason we came here.

"Yes," I tell Stephanie. "If she doesn't belong to anyone, we'll take her."

Stephanie sets up an appointment for us with the shelter's vet. The dog needs a rabies shot, a physical exam, and a signed health certificate for Customs, and then we'll be set. It all seems so simple, so right. Just like deciding not to go to Disney World.

WE NAME THE dog Chispa. Deciding on that name isn't easy. For some reason, we're unable to come to an agreement or even a compromise on what to call her. Every name Marisel suggests seems wrong to me, something that just doesn't fit the dog, and she feels the same about the names I propose. Two days into the dog name impasse, Marisel offers a new name for consideration. We're driving across the causeway from Green Beach in silence, aggravated with each other and frustrated by our inability to agree on a name for the dog.

"I thought of another name, but you're probably not going to like it."

She's probably right, but I ask anyway.

"What is it?"

"Chispa."

It's a Spanish word I've not heard before, and I like the way it sounds—Chees-pah, with the accent on the first syllable. It's different, unique . . . at least, for a dog who'll be living in New England.

"What does it mean?"

For me the meaning of the name is important, more important than the name itself.

"Little spark."

I smile, leaning over to kiss her temple.

"Little spark . . . I think that's perfect."

WE LEAVE VIEQUES on a Monday, the same day that throngs of show dog owners are flying home after a major American Kennel Club show held in San Juan. The airport terminal is filled with dogs milling around, lying under tables in restaurants, being fussed over by both owners and complete strangers. Even Chispa, who couldn't possibly look any more like a sato, is mistaken for a show dog by a passerby as we walk toward a restaurant. The man stops us and smiles, reaching down to pet Chispa's head.

"What a beautiful dog. What breed is she?"

I look at Marisel, see the mischief in her eyes. Oh, God, I think—here we go.

"She's a sato."

"A sato? I've never heard of that breed. Is it new?"

"No, but it's new to the AKC. They just decided to let satos compete in shows a few months ago."

"Oh, that's interesting. How'd she do?"

"She won the sato group."

About to blow Marisel's cover by laughing, I quickly excuse myself. As I walk away I can hear Marisel telling the man she thinks Chispa really should've won Best in Show, too. I watch from afar, wondering how she can possibly be carrying on this conversation with a straight face, and don't start walking back until I see the man move off in the direction of the gates. Marisel and Chispa head toward me and we meet halfway. They're both smiling, and Chispa's tail is wagging.

"I can't believe you told that man Chispa won the sato group."

"Why? If satos could be in the show, and they should be, she would've won. She's much prettier than any of those dogs."

I have to admit that last part is true—to my eyes, anyway.

"Come on, let's go get something to eat."

We've just finished our soup and gotten our check when an announcement comes over the loudspeakers. All dogs traveling on our flight are to be brought to a holding area, and from there they'll be loaded onto the plane together. The show dogs are VIP passengers, and the airline is doing everything possible to provide them with a safe and stress-free travel experience. Marisel gets up from her seat and starts to walk off with Chispa.

"Where are you going?"

"To that room they just told us to bring the dogs to."

"I think they meant the show dogs, not our dog."

"The announcement said all dogs, not all show dogs. Chispa's a dog, and she's on that flight, so . . ."

She has a point.

When we arrive at the holding area the dog show folks are milling around, talking with each other and making last-minute adjustments to crates, bedding, and water dishes. I remove the hanging water bowl from Chispa's crate and fill it from the nearest water fountain.

I snap the bowl back onto the side of the crate, then call Chispa over to me. She walks into the open crate with no hesitation, then turns herself around to face me. I shut the crate door and lock it, then double-check the locks. Chispa watches all of this, and I wonder what she's thinking. I reach through the grate to touch her, running the tips of my fingers along the side of her face.

"You're a good girl . . . I love you . . . Everything's going to be fine."

Given the amount of VIP care and attention these dogs are getting, I actually believe my reassurance to her. Everything will indeed be fine. The last time we'd brought a dog home from a Caribbean vacation nothing had been fine—it had barely been safe, Laika traveling in a too-small crate secured with rusty screws and heavy twine, the largest crate the tiny island shelter was able to provide, then being forced to ride in the trunk of a taxi in the late afternoon San Juan traffic and heat, the lid held open with rope. Those twenty-five minutes from Isla Grande airport to Muñoz Marin airport still rank among the most stressful of my life.

But this time around it's all good. We leave Chispa in the holding room with the other dogs and walk over to the gate area. As the dogs are being loaded onto the plane, there's a mad dash to the windows, everyone wanting to watch the unusual spectacle of crated dogs moving along a conveyor belt, one after another, up into the belly of the plane.

"There goes Blue, see him?"

"Oh, there's my dog, too, three crates behind Blue."

It reminds me of waiting for my luggage to appear on the carousel, but in reverse. And at the moment, my luggage is nowhere in sight. I look over at Marisel.

"Do you see Chispa?"

"No, but so many of those crates look alike. I have no idea how anyone can tell which one's theirs. Don't worry, Pea, she's there."

But of course, I do worry.

When we finally board and settle into our seats there's something waiting for us. At first glance it looks like a "Do Not Disturb" sign with a drawing of a dog on it. Marisel pulls it out from behind the tray table, and we see that it's got her seat number written on it, along with the words "I'm on board, too!"

I reach for Marisel's hand. We smile at each other, happy to be on our way home.

I'm convinced we'd gone to Vieques for one reason, a reason now sitting in the cargo hold of the plane in the company of some of the most pampered dogs on the planet.

Not too bad, I tell myself, for a sato dumped on a Caribbean beach to live, or die, on her own.

MARISEL AND I still joke that Chispa must have been on her very best behavior in the villa on Vieques. Each morning, she'd stand quietly outside our bedroom door, patiently waiting for us to wake up and invite her into the room with us. Instead of begging for food, she positioned herself just outside the kitchen, not venturing in unless we called her. When we ate, she sat a respectful distance away. Never once did she have an accident in the villa. She was the perfect dog.

Once home in Chelsea, though, things begin to change. Fast. She seems to understand that no matter how badly she behaves, we're not going to bring her back to Sun Bay Beach— or any other beach—and drive away. She becomes less of a Stepford dog each day, until by the end of the first week she's lying on the furniture and sleeping on our bed.

She exhibits a finely tuned instinct to identify the one person at the table who's willing to break the rules and slip her some food on the sly. No more hanging around on the periphery of kitchen and dining room for her—mealtime is serious business now, and she's right there where the action is. Outside the house, she takes an unusual liking to my red Toyota Corolla, and I often look out the dining room window into the driveway and see her sunning herself on the car's roof in the blazing heat.

She's high-spirited and full of life, and over time she accomplishes what no one else has been able to, tugging me slowly out of the depths of grief with her infectious joy. It's not long before I'm completely dependent on her presence, before I'm certain I can't possibly live without her—my unexpected savior.

TEN

IN THE DAYS that follow my previous visit to the Dog Chapel, that visit in which I contemplated joy, I experience a sense of serenity, hopeful—even certain—that the prayer I've sent out into the embrace of the Dog Chapel's sanctuary will bring some measure of joy and perhaps even peace to my suffering dog. And for a while it does. There are times when Chispa is quiet, times when she seems enlivened by and interested in Chula's presence. I learn to be grateful for these moments, especially as they become increasingly rare. Within a short time, Chispa's anxious behaviors become more frequent and pronounced, and I'm forced to acknowledge that perhaps her situation has worsened beyond the reach of prayer.

It's taken a long time for me to understand the nature of Chispa's condition, to be able to admit to myself that what's wrong with her could take her life. I couldn't face losing her, couldn't admit early on that those disturbing symptoms might have no cure. Perhaps most important, I felt the need to save her, as she'd once saved me.

But now, in the face of what I can no longer deny, I begin to take hesitating steps toward answering, or at the very least addressing, the question that refuses to stop nagging me, disturbing even my sleep: Is it time to let her go?

It's a question I've had to ask before, and one with which I always struggle. I find the responsibility of making a decision of that enormity and permanence on behalf of an adored animal overwhelming, even when the answer is—from a medical perspective, anyway—clear and absolute. But Chispa's situation is different, something with which I have no experience. This isn't about deciding to euthanize a dog at the end-stage of a terminal or acute physical illness, which is all I've ever known of euthanasia.

It's about judging cognitive quality of life, something there's no definitive way to measure in a dog.

In many ways she's as healthy as a nearly fourteen year old dog with a thyroid condition and arthritis can be, and it's difficult for me to imagine or justify putting a still relatively healthy dog down. But her mind is clearly compromised. Is it compromised enough that her life has become untenable? This is the question I turn over and over in my mind, the answer taunting me with its slipperiness. I can't seem to get a firm grasp on it, and Chispa's vets are unable to give me an opinion as to the extent of her cognitive dysfunction. The decision of whether or not to put her down will be mine and Marisel's alone.

In late February we have a discussion about it.

"Pea, I just don't think she's happy anymore . . . I think maybe it's time."

"I guess."

"Are you not sure?"

"I'm not sure at all. Part of me agrees with you, but part of me doesn't."

"What are you not sure about?"

"It's just that when I think back to Nike and Laika, or Martina and Lucy, they were all so sick. There was no doubt in my mind that letting go was the right thing to do. But I look at Chispa, and except for the fact that she has CDS, she looks basically healthy."

"I know. But I think she's having a hard time."

"I know she is . . . but is it hard enough to end her life? We don't know, not really."

We're quiet for a few minutes, taking in the implications of that thought, before I voice what's been bothering me the most, the question I now see will need to be answered before I can ever hope to make a decision.

"I'm afraid that maybe we'd be doing it for us, not for her."

"What do you mean?"

"We'd be doing it for our own sanity, because we can't stand to live with the barking anymore."

"I could never do that. I want what's best for her."

"So do I, but I don't know what that is right now."

"Then we wait. We have to be sure. I don't want you to have any regrets."

We table the discussion, but mulling it over later I begin to understand how complex the situation really is, how intertwined our life is with hers, how difficult it will be to determine what's best for Chispa alone.

And Marisel's right. There can be no regrets in this for me, not the slightest trace of guilt or second-guessing. I think back to our cat Pez's death from anaphylactic shock, precipitated by an injection of his long-time allergy medication I'd administered on the advice of a professional and against my own gut's judgment. I remember all too well the ways in which the toxic combination of regret and guilt and grief that followed his death had created a state of complete disregard for and disinterest in my own life, a dangerous state of being that had eventually required professional intervention. I don't want to travel that path again.

It's these thoughts, the recollection of a decision I'd give anything to revisit and revise, that provide the context for the situation in which I find myself now. There's a small measure of grace in knowing that this time there's complete transparency. I fully understand that one choice results in life, the other in death. Yet this knowledge makes the decision that much more difficult, the margin for error nonexistent. I have to be sure. But I have no idea what it will take for me to arrive at that point of absolute certainty.

I wonder what life is like for Chispa. Is she as anxious and distressed as her barking might lead me to believe? Or is the barking nothing more than a habit, a behavior that's become ingrained as her brain function has edged further away from normal? The possibility that she feels lost or frightened in her own home—a place in which she once moved with a taken-for-granted kind of confidence—is heartbreaking. I think back to the day we found her on Sun Bay Beach, imagine her fear and confusion at having been abandoned, and believe I'd do anything to prevent her from experiencing those feelings again.

But anything, at the moment, doesn't include putting her down. Should it? I long to be inside her head, wish for just one minute of knowing exactly what it is to be her. I wonder what she'd say to me if we shared a language beyond the simple words and gestures we use to make ourselves understood to one another. Would she say she's had enough, or would she say something else entirely?

ELEVEN

IT'S EARLY SPRING in northern New Hampshire. Mud season, the locals call it—the time of year when the snow begins to melt and the ground softens, leaving unpaved roads and driveways muddy and treacherous. It's a transitional season, a stretch of time for the hardy people who live here year-round to assess and repair winter's damages and ready their businesses for summer's tourists. Mud season is definitely not a season for tourists. It's a season for people looking for introspection and renewal . . . for people like me.

I sit on the window seat in our sunroom in Littleton, staring idly out the bay window into the woods. It's quiet right now, the kind of quiet that's long since disappeared from life in Medford but somehow finds its way into existence here. For reasons I don't understand, Chispa rarely barks in this house. It's as if an invisible force of calm settles over her when we arrive and disappears the moment she walks out the door and gets into the car. I wonder if she experiences the actual physical space of the house differently, perhaps finds comfort in the smallness of the rooms. Our house in Medford is bigger, with an open floor plan that makes the space feel larger than it actually is. Does the openness of where we live contribute to her anxiety, while the cocooning feeling of the New Hampshire house is interpreted as safe?

I've passed the point of trying to make sense of it all. I simply know that for whatever reason she is quiet here, and I'm grateful for the reprieve. I turn my gaze from the woods toward Chispa. She's sleeping soundly on the futon couch beside the window seat. I watch her breathe, marvel at the miracle of life, how simple it all seems—breathe in, breathe out, and for as long as you do this, there's life. She seems so normal in these moments of sleep that I can almost trick myself into believing there's nothing wrong.

I watch as a dream takes shape in her mind, her paws mimicking the motion of running. I wonder what's going on in her dream—is she running after Laika or Chula, or in pursuit of a squirrel or butterfly? Does her mind experience her dreams in the ways it once did? I don't know, but whatever adventure her dreaming mind has created for her, I hope it makes her happy.

I have a strong urge to stretch out next to her on the futon, to wrap my arms tightly around her warm and familiar dog body and hold her close. Instead, I remain seated in the embrace of the bay window, wanting to let Chispa have her dream, hoping it allows her to be, if only in sleep, herself. I turn away from her and gaze down the yard to the pond, my eyes focused on nothing in particular, and it's then that I see them. Laika trotting briskly out ahead, Chispa a bit behind her, hurrying to catch up. They're heading toward the pond. Ghost dogs.

I catch a glimpse of the tall green reeds that grow along the edge of the pond, and know it's summer. Laika is hot, and I watch her approach the pond with purpose, walking into the water without hesitation. The water in most areas of the pond is shallow, and she wades in to the deeper middle until the water reaches her belly. It's apparently too lazy a day for swimming. She simply stands still, enjoying the cooling relief of the water.

Chispa doesn't go in the water, not at first. She stands by the edge of the pond, then begins to pace around the perimeter, whining. She wants to be with Laika, but not in the water. She wants Laika out of the water, right now, and the whining is quickly replaced with a staccato barking: her "demand" bark. Laika is oblivious, focused on nothing but the delicious sensation of cool water on warm, bare skin. Chispa eventually realizes that no amount of barking is going to convince Laika to come out of the pond. Slowly, as if unsure of herself, she makes her way into the water until she's standing beside Laika. And then, as suddenly as they appear, they're both gone. It's another day now—a day in early spring, a day when the water in the middle of the pond is glazed over by a thin sheet of melting ice.

It takes a while for the vision of Laika and Chispa in the pond to leave me. I sit with it, watching it become one memory, then another. Laika and Chispa off-leash in the snow on the Kilburn Crags trail, Marisel and I trudging along behind them, the flapping of our snowshoe tails punctuating every step. The two of them in summer and fall on the nearby dirt road with the panoramic mountain and river views I always wished they could appreciate, racing up ahead of us but never out of sight. Tails wagging and noses to the ground as we walk them on-leash along the side of the road near the house, where they can't get enough of the moose, deer, groundhog, and bear smells that seem to reside on every blade of grass. I understand that my dogs will always live in this house, on this land, know that I'll see them everywhere I look for as long as we make our home here. Perhaps they'll even continue to return, paying an occasional visit to those who'll live here long after we've moved away. The idea of this makes me smile.

When Chispa wakes up I put her leash on and take her outside. I'm hoping she might want to walk down to the pond, but no. She's moving stiffly, and only goes as far as it takes her to find an acceptable patch of ground to pee on. She's usually finicky about this, but not today. She finds her spot quickly, then turns around and heads back toward the porch, walking up the four steps slowly, but on her own. Inside, I give her a couple of dog biscuits, which she devours enthusiastically. She spends several minutes drinking at the water bowl, then returns to her place on the futon and falls asleep again.

The house resonates with an unfamiliar quiet. It's the kind of quiet that echoes with its own stillness, the kind of quiet that connects me with myself in a profound way and opens up an uncluttered space for contemplation. And in that space, I become aware of something both important and surprising—I

understand, in a flashing, visceral insight that defies being held
or examined, that I will never be able to separate what's best
for me from what's best for Chispa, and that it doesn't matter.
This isn't the work I need to do, the question I need to answer.

The real question is about the soul, about the essence of
what makes each living being who they are. Does a disease like
dementia cause little bits and pieces of that essence to disin-
tegrate over time, until eventually life is distilled to nothing
more than the physical machinations of living, the in and out
of the breath, the feeding and hydration of the body? What,
exactly, is the essence of Chispa's spirit—or, for that matter, of
any dog's spirit? And if it's gone, or nearly so, is life no longer
worth living? I decide to make a visit to the Dog Chapel for
some guidance from the kindred spirits who've unknowingly
become my most important support system in my struggle to
decide whether or not it's time to let Chispa go.

The following morning I drive to the Dog Chapel alone.
I want to be able to take as much time as I need to read the
notes in the chapel, to let the thoughts and experiences of
others who've been where I am now seep into the quiet space
that's opened up within me and, hopefully, turn my questions
into answers.

As I approach the open door and hear the familiar notes of
the music, I realize how much a part of me this place is now,
how dependent I've become on the peace I find here. Once
inside the chapel, I immediately sense another presence. It's a
human presence, and I walk into the sanctuary expecting to
see a person sitting quietly in prayer. But there's no one there.

I sit in the pew I now consider mine, a pew I've sat in so
many times that I imagine it must by now have absorbed the
sweat and warmth and energy from my body into its own
form. Breathing deeply, I attempt to prepare myself for the
always emotional experience of reading the notes on the walls,
and for whatever answer I may find among them today. As my
breathing slows and quiets, the feeling that there's someone sitting in the pew with me becomes stronger. I don't understand

it, as I'm clearly alone in the chapel, and begin to wonder if perhaps the stress of my life over the past year is now manifesting itself in a new and strange way.

After a few moments of intent focus on the in and out of my breath, I feel centered, prepared to immerse myself in the words of love, life, and loss splashed across the chapel on those bright little post-its. I get up and walk back into the vestibule, accompanied by a strong sensation of being followed.

"What is wrong with you," I chide myself. "There's obviously no one else here."

And then it clicks.

The presence I feel with me in the chapel is Stephen Huneck. Stephen, who ended his life with a shot to the head in early January, just a little over two months ago. I remember coming across his obituary in the online version of the *Boston Globe*, remember still the absolute shock of it. How could this have happened, how could he be gone? Heartbreaking, inexplicable, that a person with such gifts could be lost to the world.

What could possibly have led this man, who'd once nearly succumbed to life-threatening illness, who'd survived not so much through the marvels of modern medicine as through the miracle of love, who understood perhaps better than most the value of life, to decide he was done with it? Whatever it was must certainly have been beyond his ability to bear, for even one more second.

I never met Stephen, though I'd often contemplated seeking him out in his studio and asking him if, when he was building the Dog Chapel and creating the artwork that fills it, he'd ever envisioned what it would become—a fluid and interactive memorial, a place of pilgrimage to so many seekers. Now I wish I had. Still, I feel his gentle, loving energy beside me as I move through the chapel and realize that in a way completely defying rational articulation, I've been given the chance to meet him after all.

I begin to slowly make the rounds, starting with the walls in the vestibule. I read many old and familiar notes and search

for those that are new, those that might hold some part of the
larger answer to my questions. I don't expect to find the answer
in one place. Instead, I assume it will formulate itself from
a line here, another line or two there. And I have what feels
like all the time in the world to search, to discover what I'm
looking for. After some time in the vestibule, I move into the
sanctuary. For some reason, this is where I seem to find most
of the words that speak to me.

> "Dear Kira, You were Julie's rock, so solid, so sure,
> irreplaceable. Your strength made all of us
> stronger. You gave us everything you had, and we
> are forever indebted."

> "Sugar—The day you passed I cried—not because
> I was sad to see you leave us, but because I was so
> blessed to have had you in my life. You will always
> be remembered as the gentle 'Nanny Dog' of the
> neighborhood. Easter and Halloween will never
> be quite as much fun without you. I will always
> remember your sweet nature and unconditional
> love."

> "Madison taught us the meaning of unconditional
> love. She brought a kind of joy into our lives that
> we hadn't known. She inspired us to live life to
> the fullest, with love and kindness as our guiding
> force."

> "Harley, you were my best friend. Thank you for
> teaching me about life. We went through so much
> together. I will miss your love and devotion until
> the day I die. Momma will see you some day and
> we will be together again. I love you, Harley girl."

> "Old Dear Pepper: No more falling down the stairs
> for you."

This note in particular causes me to choke up, its summary of the devastations of age, of all it steals from us, so vivid and succinct. I wish—for what is certainly more than the hundredth time—for the long years of a human lifetime to share with my dogs, rather than the cruelly truncated canine lifetime.

And then I come across a different kind of note—a signed note written in list form on stationery, left by a veterinarian named Joy Lucas for her dog Zu.

> "To affect one's core.
> To inspire a career.
> To fill one's heart with love and confidence.
> To bestow undying loyalty.
> To save one's life.
> Not the role of kings but that of a dog.
> Until we join as constant companions."

This short, powerful list of sentence fragments speaks to what many consider the heart of the human-canine relationship, and, by association, the essence of a dog itself: dogs, through their unconditional love, friendship, and unwavering devotion, ultimately teach us how to be better people, and in doing so change us, often quite literally saving our lives. This is who a dog is, what sharing a life with a dog means.

But what of the dog in relationship to other dogs, the natural world, herself? What is the essence of a dog's spirit when not considered or viewed solely through the lens of the human-canine relationship? I think it's probably best understood through play.

The walls of the Dog Chapel are filled with notes about play, and I find it both interesting and telling that it's these notes that create for me the most vivid mental pictures of who a dog was and how he engaged with the world, these notes that provide me with the clearest window into the unique spirit of the dog for whom they were written.

"Trucker loved cold weather and snow so he would prance as he rubbed his nose through the freshly fallen snow."

"I'll always remember this about Millie: Loved to read. Loved Christmas. She is my 'baby.' She loved Mollie. Loved to play ball."

"Tasha. Heart dog, best friend. Walking, running, hiking, road trips, swimming, and tennis balls. Our happy dance! Dance my sweet angel! I love you the best."

I return to my pew and sit, letting the words I've spent the past three hours reading separate and settle. As they do, images of Chispa appear, clicking through my mind rapidly, a high-speed slide show with no pause button—the ways in which she's affected my own core, filled my own heart with love, been as loyal a friend as I could ever hope to have, saved me from despair, and played with a joyful abandon I could only envy, never emulate.

I see her lying at my feet on a chaise on Green Beach in Vieques two days after we found each other, barking loudly at an approaching stranger, even then my fierce protector. In the next image she's in the yard in New Hampshire, leaping through the air chasing after a small cloud of migrating butterflies. Now I see her looking out the living room window in Chelsea, barking furiously at her nemesis Sinbad, a large, gentle, brindle mixed breed who completely ignores her as he walks nonchalantly by with his person. And then there's image after image of her lying or sitting beside me, her body melting into mine, her head resting in my lap.

But as these images fade away, others, not so happy, appear. I see her lying on the chaise in the living room in Medford, barking endlessly. I watch as she walks in circles around her own home as if she has no idea where she is or how to navigate the once so-familiar rooms. Now she gazes at me, chin resting on the edge of her nest bed, that wonderful bed we saw and fell in love with in a shop on Main Street in Littleton, a bed woven together with branches to look like a bird nest for a dog. The expression in those deep brown eyes that once held so much joy and intelligence and life is dull, deadened.

There's just enough time to focus on each image. Not enough time to fully absorb it, but enough to understand in a down-to-the-bones way who my dog was, the ways in which she's changed, and who she is now. I'm left with a terrible suffocating feeling, a sensation of being trapped inside something invisible, and it's then that I know. This is how Chispa experiences her world now.

Tomorrow, I'll call Bari and tell her it's time.

The Word of Dog
PLAY

"Dear Bandit: I loved my dog very much! He died 2 weeks ago. He liked to bark at bigger dogs and roll in the carpet and grunt. He lived a long and happy life. We will miss him so much."

"Teasel—my boy forever—You ran joyfully on Dog Mountain, now in heaven."

"Haleigh Maria Louise—You were such a good puppy always wanting to play and always wanting belly rubs. I love u and miss you with all my heart."

"Bella—Springer Spaniel: Loved balls, sticks, or anything that you could throw."

"This is about our dog Lucy—she was a good dog. She was a good writer. She loved Nancy and Torben. And Lucy loved dog biscuits & also liked to have birthday parties. The End. Woof."

"Darby, my sweet 'Boo,' I love you & miss you very much! 'Tomorrow' never came for you on 7/10/06. I will never forget our last game of fetch—you died doing something you loved & in my arms. Rest well my special girl until we meet again at the Bridge."

"Opus, may you chase rabbits all day long."

"Tinker—best little lollipop eating dog ever!"

"Mango & Bunny—Dogs of our hearts always.
Sweet girls—I know you're hiking together in the
sky. Thanks for all your love!"

"Ms. Emily will always be remembered as the tree
climbing, car jumping shadow who grew up with
me. She will always be remembered & missed by
myself and the many squirrels she almost caught."

TWELVE

AS THINGS TURN out, I don't call Bari the next day. In fact, I don't call her for another two months. I don't call her because suddenly, inexplicably, Chispa seems better. Not better in the sense that she's well, but better in that her symptoms seem less pronounced—still there, but not intolerable. I remind myself that I'm judging the severity of her symptoms from my perspective, that I have no idea to what extent she finds them tolerable. I urge myself to remember the lessons of my last visit to the Dog Chapel, the conclusion I arrived at there: It's time.

But once back home in Medford after the weekend away, everything that seemed so right while I stood in the Dog Chapel is thrown into question. All the words that spoke to me so clearly just a day before seem to vanish from my mind as if they'd never existed.

Chispa's Monday morning walk is what changes everything, what brings me from "It's time" to "Not yet." For the first time in over two months, she trots along beside me and Chula, down the front steps, out of the cul-de-sac, onto Doonan Street. We approach the place where she usually stops, refusing to walk further. But on this morning she seems not to recognize that place, walks right by it. Her tail, so often down in recent months, wags back and forth, her nose actively sniffing the scents around her.

We near Laika's tree, a late-leafing maple Laika had never been able to pass by without pulling off the sidewalk for a lengthy sniff of the soil around its base, of the trunk as high up as her nose could reach. Who knew what scents congregated at and on this particular tree, or why, but she found them fascinating. One day, stopped at the tree, I'd noticed that a tuft of her fur was loose, sticking up like a tiny peak of meringue.

I gently removed the little clump of silky gold from her body, and then tucked it into the notch at the base of the tree's trunk, a little piece of its most ardent fan. Today, Chispa decides she'd like to pay Laika's tree a visit, so we stop while she sniffs around for a bit, and then move on.

I'm astonished by the change in her demeanor, by her desire to continue walking. I grasp the obvious metaphor in this, see it as absolute confirmation of her desire to hang on to her life just a little longer. To me, this trumps everything, including the emotional shift recently experienced in the Dog Chapel. If Chispa wants more of her life, who am I to refuse it? It's her life, not mine. I'm simply the guardian of that life this time around. And so we walk, the three of us, the full distance of our normal route. When we return home, Marisel is fully dressed, car keys in hand.

"What happened, Pea? You were gone for so long I was just about to get in the car and go look for you. I thought something might've happened to Chispa . . ."

I hear the fear in her voice, the uncertainty, the way in which these emotions have woven themselves so firmly into the framework of our lives. I hold her tightly and try to kiss the fear out of her.

"She wanted to walk—we went the entire way, down and back. Her tail wagged, she stopped to sniff at Laika's tree . . . I don't know what this is about, but it's amazing."

Marisel stares at Chispa, who's now digging a bit at the blankets in the nest bed, making a brief attempt at arranging them to her satisfaction before settling herself down.

"Unbelievable . . ."

She walks over to the nest bed, kneels down beside it, and kisses Chispa's head. She murmurs a short monologue into Chispa's fur between kisses. The only words I catch are "you're my good, good girl . . . *que buena.*" She looks up at me.

"Are you still going to call Bari today?"

"No. I think we should give it more time. I don't think Chispa's ready yet."

"Neither am I."

And now, neither am I.

I OFTEN WONDER what brings Chispa back in time that morning in early spring, if only for a short time. Is it the aftereffects of the calming time spent in New Hampshire? Is it the slight warming of the air, the special smell that appears at this time of year, the smell that holds the sure promise of new life? Or do her bones simply stop aching, for whatever reason, long enough for a week of walks? Is it a shift in body, mind, or both? I don't know, but whatever the cause of this remission, I feel blessed by its existence.

She still barks, still paces, but it all seems less onerous now. In reality it's not, but I allow myself to see it as such. A week goes by, and then, suddenly, it's as if the previous seven days never happened.

On the eighth day, as we approach her former stop-and-take-me-home place, I fully expect to keep right on going. Things are different on our walks now, nearly normal. But suddenly something in her memory kicks in, or maybe she just doesn't feel like walking. Whatever the reason, Chispa stops and refuses to budge. I've never seen a living being so immovable. No amount of cajoling on my part will make her take another step forward. The only step she's willing to take is the one that turns her around and heads her in the direction of home. And so we go, Chula whining over the early end to her walk.

"It's okay, Chula—we'll go back out in a few minutes."

My voice has that happy, high-pitched tone I use when I want my dogs to know it's all good. Especially when it's not. We reach the front steps and Chispa makes a sudden break for the door. I'm not expecting this change of pace, and I'm pulled off balance, nearly falling up the concrete steps. Once we're inside I unhook her leash, and she immediately goes to the chaise, climbs onto it, and lies down. In the time it takes me to walk into the kitchen, get her treat out of the ceramic jar, and walk back into the living room, she's sound asleep. I slip the treat into the pocket of my jacket and pick up the end of Chula's leash.

"C'mon, Bug, let's go."

CHISPA NEVER GOES for a long walk again. Some days she doesn't even make it beyond the end of the cul-de-sac. Whatever occurred during that week back in the very early spring is gone, and the only joy I'm able to discern in her existence is her ever present, clear enjoyment of food. I understand, on a logical, objective level, that her symptoms are slightly worse than when I'd made the decision a month and a half ago that it was time to let her go. Following this logical and objective line of thinking, it should be obvious to me that if it was time then, it's beyond time now. But somehow, it's not obvious.

Instead, I keep asking myself "what if?" What if she has another remission, or whatever that short period of engagement with her world was? What if it's longer this time? What if, by some miracle, my prayers for her are finally answered? Those seven days in which hope obliterated reason have changed everything, set me back light years. It feels impossible to return to the point of sanity and peace I found in the Dog Chapel, that moment of complete trust in my decision to let my sweet dog go, with grace and dignity and love. Now I question everything, replacing reality with possibility, what is with what could be. *Could be*—but only if Chispa is still alive.

I'm stuck in this place, as immovable as Chispa when she reaches that particular patch of sidewalk near the corner of Sawyer and Doonan and refuses to take another step forward. I'm no longer ready to concede, to admit there's nothing more to be done. My inability to accept the reality of the situation becomes a source of friction between me and Marisel, who's reached the point of being certain it's time for us to see Chispa out of this life.

"I thought you were feeling sure about putting her down."

"I was, but that was before. Before whatever that week was."

"I know . . . that made it harder for me, too. But whatever that was is gone, and she's worse now, not better."

"She's not worse—she's just the same."

"Pea. She's not."

"But she was better for a while. What if she gets better again? And what if there's something else we can try?"

What if, what if, what if.

"Didn't the neurologist at Angell say that if Anipryl didn't work there wasn't really anything else to try?"

I stare across the kitchen table at her, wondering who she is.

"I can't let her go without trying every possible option. Can you?"

"No. It's just that I think we've done everything there is to do."

THIRTEEN

I EVENTUALLY COME to realize that the real issue for me isn't that I think there's anything more to be done for Chispa. That's simply the tangible way in which the actual issue is manifested—something specific to point to and say, "There. That's what it's all about." But what it's really about is something far more complex, something grounded in a combination of hope and responsibility that's taken on a life of its own.

I understand that I'm stuck because I can't let go of hope. What I don't understand, what I've never been able to learn, is how to do so. Two years earlier, when Tomas was ill, Marisel and I experienced the wild roller coaster ride of hope and despair that comes with loving a person suffering from dementia. It was a draining experience, but we nevertheless chose to get on that same ride over and over again, drawn by the power of hope like hummingbirds to the color red.

Now my dog has dementia, and hope once again dangles itself before me, tantalizing in its possibilities for Chispa's recovery. I reach out and grab it, refuse to let go. But Marisel, who loves Chispa just as much as I do, feels differently. This time, influenced by the last months of Tomas's life, she holds onto hope for only a short while before releasing it. I'm angry and upset with her, feeling left alone in my belief that it's too soon to let Chispa go. I'm also upset with myself. Why can't things be as clear for me as they are for Marisel? Why can't I, too, just let go?

I turn these questions over and over in my mind before the answer becomes apparent: I can't let go of hope because, from the moment Chispa's eyes and mine locked, in the split second before she jumped through the car door I held open for her on that narrow, dusty road leading out of Sun Bay Beach, I've felt

responsible for saving Chispa's life. But this answer leads me
to ask another, more existential question: *What does it mean to
save a life?*

Some time ago I assisted with the teaching of Death and
Dying in Life and Literature at Harvard Divinity School. I
thought that being immersed in the exercise of reading and
discussing the literature of death and dying might enable me
to look at death more objectively, perhaps even learn to
experience it more as friend than foe.

Although death has yet to become my friend, I've come to
appreciate that dying—the period of time leading up to the
moment in which the last breath is exhaled—holds enormous
possibilities for living. We're still alive throughout the process
of our dying, alive right up until the moment we're not. And
so making it possible for those we love to die what palliative
care specialist Dr. Ira Byock refers to as a "good death," a death
in which the process of dying enables us to hold on to who
we are, to live as authentically as possible until we're dead, is
lifesaving. I want Chispa to die a good death, and wonder now
if perhaps I've let things go too far, let her drift too far beyond
her authentic self.

But I find it complicated, this matter of deciding when it's
time to let another life go, a life that belongs to me only in the
sense that I've agreed to be its steward. And that's the sticking
point—because I've made the commitment to care for Chispa,
to be responsible for all aspects of her life, I'm ultimately
responsible for making the decision to end that life, the same
life I've so tenderly and faithfully nurtured for so many years.
It's a responsibility I've never felt completely comfortable
accepting on behalf of any of the animals with whom I've
shared my life, even when I've known with absolute certainty
that it was the only right and loving choice to make. And I
certainly don't feel comfortable accepting it now, when the
parameters for decision making seem to shift daily.

I don't have to make the decision, of course. I could leave
it up to her, let her own body decide when it's time to die.

But I don't feel entirely comfortable with this approach either, believe that letting her go on until her mind stops telling her body to eat and breathe will likely rob her of the opportunity to die as well as possible. And do I have any more right to make that decision on her behalf than I do to make the decision to end her life? I want to do right by her, but, stuck within the murk of it all, I can't see my way clear to knowing what that is. Is it right, morally and ethically, to end the life of a dog whose mind is clearly compromised but whose body isn't ready to die? I flip the question on its side, examine it from a different perspective: If I could have made the decision to end Tomas's life, would I have chosen to do so?

I'm surprised by the ease with which I answer this morally fraught question—yes, I would have, without hesitation. And while his body was much further down the path of deterioration than Chispa's, my answer has nothing to do with the state of his body and everything to do with the state of his mind. To see this intelligent and thoughtful man, so gifted with the written and spoken word, an orator at Masons meetings and at our holiday dinner table, no longer able to understand or speak either English or Spanish—of all his symptoms, this alone would have been enough.

I wasn't given the option to help Tomas die with the dignity of authentic living. And if I'm completely honest, I have to admit that I'm not entirely sure he would have chosen this option for himself. A deeply religious man, I think he might have chosen instead to put his trust in God, to have faith that whatever the process of his dying, this was what was written in his book of days. But I do have the option, socially and legally sanctioned, to choose death for Chispa, to decide that her life is no longer tenable. It's a true and generous gift, this option, yet it's a gift I'm still not able to accept with either graciousness or gratitude.

FOURTEEN

MIDWAY THROUGH the following week, Marisel and I decide to drive up to Littleton for the weekend. Every time we travel to New Hampshire now, I wonder if this will be the last time Chispa walks into the house, the last time she sits in the window seat surveying the yard, her northern kingdom. There are moments now when I feel so close to being ready to let her go, to acknowledging that my responsibility is to her soul, not her body. But when I conjure up these "last time" images of her in the places she's loved so much, I'm overcome by the finality of it all and find myself unable to contemplate her death. I try not to visualize these images, but it's difficult.

It's May now. Mud season has come and gone and spring has finally arrived in the mountains. The leaves on the shade trees are open, their green the color of fresh new life. Every last trace of snow has disappeared from the ground, not to return for another five months, maybe six. The hard brown earth has turned soft and lush, and everywhere the birds sing. Soon the lupines will bloom, riotous fields of pink, white, and every shade of purple imaginable. The black flies will arrive soon too, but it seems a small price to pay for such loveliness.

On Sunday I head off by myself to the Dog Chapel, hoping to find whatever it was I'd found there the last time—the time I left feeling so at peace with my decision to end Chispa's life. For the first time, I feel a sense of something close to fear as I walk across the gallery lawn toward the chapel. I've come here to find whatever it is that will enable me to let go of Chispa, to believe, with not one lingering doubt, that it's the right thing to do.

Yet for as much as I hope to find the words, or strength, or divine inspiration that will free me to move forward, I fear that moment of discovery, the relinquishment and subsequent grief it will ultimately represent. I quicken my pace, as if by doing so I might leave my fear behind, but it accompanies me like a shadow as I walk up the granite steps of the Dog Chapel.

Once inside the vestibule, though, all fear vanishes. The four walls of this chapel seem to have some sort of magical power over me, some psychic energy that generates a sensation of calm, peace, and profound love. I take a deep breath, an inhalation exhaled as unexpected tears—the kind of tears that happen when taking communion after a long, long time away from God, the kind of tears you cry when you know that, finally, you've come home.

I begin my journey along the walls of the Dog Chapel, starting with the vestibule and eventually moving into the Sanctuary. I take my time. So many of the notes and pictures on the wall are familiar to me now, and I revisit them as if they were old friends, the names of the dogs almost as dear to me as the names of my own dogs. Kodiak, Autumn, Sadie, Amber, Toby . . . you were loved beyond what you could imagine, and are missed more than you will ever know. Soon Chispa's name will join theirs, and perhaps one day someone will take a measure of comfort from the love note I'll leave for her, posted with a pushpin on some tiny patch of wall, the words and emotions overlapping with those that surround it.

Every so often I come across a note that's unfamiliar to me. Are these notes newly written, or have I simply missed them in my previous visits? Either is possible, but I'm grateful for these new-to-me words. I need something I've not seen before, something that will cause the emotional shift I've come here to find—the shift that will set both me and Chispa free. As is so often the case when I visit the Dog Chapel, I don't know what I'm looking for. But I do know I'll recognize it when I see it.

It's not long before I discover it: six pages of letters to one beloved dog. I recognize the dog's name—Zu. And I recognize the note on top. It's a note I'd read during an earlier visit, the one written by veterinarian Joy Lucas, the one that had helped me understand the true essence of a dog's spirit. It was this note that had once brought me to the brink of certainty, confident that it was time to lead Chispa gently into the new life that awaited her. To the brink, but not beyond. As I remove the pushpin affixing the stack of letters to the wall and hold the weight of this woman's words in my hands, I instinctively know that this time will be different.

The paper on which the letters to Zu are written feels hand-made, the ragged edges of each page slightly different from the next. It's lovely, and I imagine Joy picking it out especially to write these letters for her dog, the most beautiful paper for her most adored Zu. I take the letters over to my pew and sit down to read them. The first letter, the one beneath the note I've already read, is written in 2007, five years after Zu's death.

"It's been 5 long years since your passing. Some days it feels like yesterday, others it feels like 30 years. My heart still aches to have you by my side. Time has taken the memory of your smell and the sound of your feet. I wouldn't have traded anything for the 10 years I spent in your friendship and I eagerly await seeing you again someday. My loyal friend, my constant companion, you remain in my heart."

I want to know this woman, want to rush home, Google her name, call or e-mail her. She'd understand me, I tell myself, names in her words that thing which, along with fear, is at the core of my reluctance to let go—the inevitable fact that time will eventually render inaccessible the kind of memories so tightly held onto in the days and weeks after a dog's death. The way Chispa smells, an odd aroma like Fritos corn chips. The sound of her steps across the wooden floors. The tone and pitch of her bark . . . ultimately, they'll all disappear, the human brain incapable of indefinite retention of those sensory memories. I'll be unable to conjure these aspects of her physical being any longer; will have to be content with feeling her presence in my heart, right alongside the dull ache of grief that will also reside there, permanently etched into muscle memory.

I turn this page over and place it beside me on the pew. The next letter is dated 6-26-02, and is three pages long. It's written during the very last days of Zu's life, as the woman who loves him watches him sleep. I begin to read, but my vision blurs within the first few lines. Joy's love for Zu is so deep, her grief at his impending death so gut wrenching, that for a moment I'm not sure I can bear witness to it. I'm tempted to just leave the letter on the pew beside me, run out of the chapel, and drive away.

But I don't.

I read on, even as my tears make doing so nearly impossible. While our circumstances are different, I understand this woman—know what it is to love a dog in this profound, all-encompassing way, to love a dog more than oneself. I understand her love, her loss, her grief. And in the next section of the letter, I understand why I came here today, why I stood right in front of these particular words, saw them for the very first time in a place where words are sometimes buried three layers deep.

"You have not only helped me save lives, but you have saved mine as well. I was able to return the gift to you once. This is beyond my powers. I cannot give you that gift again. As your Mom and veterinarian, that kills me . . . I will try to be strong for you, and to plan our parting beautifully. This is the hardest thing I've had to endure. But don't be afraid. You won't be alone. Many good animal friends have gone before you. And I promise you will be the first person I look for when I join you in heaven."

In reading these words, I feel the weight of heavy emotion begin to lift, a slow, steady rising that begins deep within the center of my body and continues upward through my chest and neck and head before exiting my body into the silence of the Dog Chapel sanctuary.

"*This is beyond my powers.*"

What must it take for a veterinarian to speak those words, to admit powerlessness in the face of the illness that will steal her dog from her? I think of all the times I've wished I were a vet in the past year. Those times are countless, the wish grounded in the irrational belief that if only I were a vet, I'd know what to do for Chispa, know how to reverse her illness, how to save her life. Never mind that not one of the vets I've taken her to has been able to do the impossible. If I were a vet, I'd somehow be able to make that kind of magic happen.

But sitting in my pew in the Dog Chapel, hands folded on top of the stack of letters to Zu arranged neatly on my lap, I understand that nothing I could have been, or said, or done would have changed the outcome. A vet possesses no more magical powers than I, and for a brief moment I wonder how it is that I'm just now realizing this.

I've been transformed by this stranger's words, by her ability to admit powerlessness over her dog's illness. And there's something else, too. For the first time, I understand that I've been asking myself the wrong question. The question isn't, "How can I save Chispa's life?" The real question, the one I should have been asking all along, is, "How can I help her die?" My task is not to find some non-existent treatment or medication to prolong her physical life, but to release her soul to life everlasting.

I feel every last remnant of guilt, fear, and hope that has prevented me from letting go of Chispa dissipate. I know now, with absolute certainty, that which has been obvious for quite some time, obvious to everyone but me: it's time.

In my newfound state of emotional clarity, I understand Chispa's vocalizing for what it is—the sense of being lost in the world, and the fear that accompanies this experience. No, my dog isn't physically broken down, not in need of hospitalization or life-support measures. But she is, in fact, ill. And she's suffering. I see this now, know it to be true. For a brief moment I allow myself to wallow yet again in the injustice of it, that this loving dog with her unique personality has spent the last months of her life in this way. Why my dog? She doesn't deserve it.

But as I look around at the writing on the walls, my existential self-indulgence is short-lived. Each of the dogs whose photographs surround me, whose lives are born witness to in snippets of love and devotion and grief, are as unique and beloved as my own. I have no idea how most of them died, but assume many suffered from chronic or terminal illness. I imagine their pain, imagine their families going through the same emotional struggles that have consumed me for the past year and especially the last five months. My question becomes something altogether different: Why *not* my dog?

I get up from the pew and walk over to where I found the letters to Zu. I return them to their place on the wall, knowing I will be forever indebted to the woman who wrote them. I think that I really will look her up one day, let her know how much those words meant to me, how they freed me to do right by my own dog. It's all still too close to the bone for me, but some day.

For now, I'll go home and tell Marisel it's time to let our girl go. Tomorrow morning I'll call Bari. And in whatever short time remains with Chispa, I'll love her. Just that. I can't do anything more.

Like most people who've come before me in the Dog Chapel, I believe in life after death. And so I trust . . . trust that when Chispa's spirit leaves her body, she'll perhaps linger for a moment to take one last look at the two women who love her with their whole hearts and the vet who so competently and affectionately cared for her up until the very end. And then her spirit will fly, up and out of the hospital she hates, soaring until it reaches the place where she'll be free, finally and forever, of all that ails her.

The Word of Dog
TRUST

"Dear Boys, You changed my life in ways wonderful and unexpected. You taught me about loyalty, life, love, and play. Sadly some of these disappeared from my life when you disappeared from my life. Every day you suffered, I suffered. Every day you were happy made me more happy. You cannot imagine how missed you are. Not a day, minute, or second goes by that you are not in my thoughts. All we have left are urns full of ashes. Though they may be small they contain a universe. It is a universe I hope to be part of someday. Be rest assured we will meet and be together again. Peyote, we will swim, play ball, and run. Fido, you will walk without a leash, steal cheese and butter. We will rub our backs together again."

"Miss Zoe—I am so sorry that we had to say good bye so early. I know that you will be waiting with a Frisbee at the rainbow bridge. We will always love you!"

"Cali, I will never forget your smell, your bark, your strong spirit. You were such a fresh girl. I was honored to enter into your life and into your heart the last couple years of your life. Thank you for letting me in. I will see you again someday. Please take care of Harley for me. Tell her I love her. I love you, Cal Cal."

"Dearest Jessie, Enjoy the hiking trails in heaven, until we meet again. Then we will walk them together. We love you!"

"Dutchess—6 years ago you left us with the look of understanding in your eyes. We all miss you so much. Anthony really missed you—all those years of growing up with you by his side. He always said 'If my Dutchie dies I'm going with her.' He must have known something we didn't because not even two months later God took Anthony from us also in a car accident. But of course you know that don't you girl because the two of you are up there making mischief aren't you. We miss you both with all our hearts! Rest in peace and wait for us! Love you."

"RIP Rudy—He was the spitting image of Toto, more fun than a barrel of flying monkeys, and more stubborn than the Wicked Witch. He had heart, courage, and brains and he's now somewhere over the rainbow. He left us way too early and I miss the little guy a lot."

"I am certain that just after he passed I could hear him barking for attention, as we sat down for dinner. I was afraid to tell my wife but she later confided in me she heard his barks as well when she came to the dinner table. With that . . . I am certain he is in heaven, also certain that when my wife and I slip over the boundaries that divide heaven and earth, Sam will be there to welcome us home again."

FIFTEEN

I DON'T MENTION the vet's long love letter when I arrive home from the Dog Chapel. Instead, I take Chispa and Chula out onto the back deck with me to sit in the afternoon sunshine. I want to stare at the mountains across the river for a while, need the solace of knowing that God does indeed create some things that live on, perhaps forever. At this time next week, when I return to New Hampshire with my world forever changed and everything within me feeling shattered and shredded, these mountains will still be here, visible from nearly every room in the house, providing silent testament to strength and solidity, to the possibility of survival.

Still, I try not to look that far ahead. Instead I try to focus on the here and now, on the bodies of my dogs stretched out across the deck's warm and weathered floorboards. I notice the deepening of their breathing as the sun soaks into their bones and splashes light across their fur. I notice how normal Chispa looks, no different than the hundreds of other times she's laid on the same small patch of deck floor, her front paws crossed in that familiar position, dainty and lady-like. I notice the floorboards need scraping and a new coat of varnish.

My mind wanders back to the Dog Chapel, and I reflect on what makes this tiny church such a place of transformation for me as I recall a conversation I once had there with a man named Tim.

WHEN I FIRST see Tim, I'm intrigued. He looks nothing like anyone I've ever met in the Dog Chapel—he's big and burly and bearded, long reddish hair pulled into a ponytail, purple paisley bandana wrapped around his head. His Harley-Davidson shirt is visible through his open leather biker's jacket. The man's tough mountain-man-cum-biker persona seems so out of place against the backdrop of emotional words on the walls surrounding him—until I say hello. Until he says hello. Until I hear the sorrow in his voice.

"I lost my old boy Jackson a little over a year ago," he tells me.

"I'm sorry. I know how hard it is to lose them . . . and the pain never really goes away. Not completely, anyway. At least, not for me."

"Yeah. It hurts like nothing else. You love them so much, and then they're gone."

"I know exactly what you mean."

He smiles at me. "I know you do. Everybody here does," he adds, gesturing at the chapel walls. "That's why I come to this place, because people here understand. They get that love, that pain."

"Do you come here often?"

"Whenever I can."

"Me too."

"I'm Tim. Nice to meet you."

I shake his outstretched hand. "Gail; same."

"Well, I think I'll sit down and say a prayer for Jackson and then head out. Nice meeting you."

"Likewise."

And then, almost as an afterthought, he says something else, something that resonates deeply.

"You know, there's something about this place that makes me feel close to him, like he's with me. It's another reason I come here."

"I feel the same way—like my dogs' spirits are here in the sanctuary, right beside me."

"What were their names?"

"Comet and Nike."

"Well, consider a prayer for them said."

I reach over and hug this bear of a man, do it without a second thought. In other circumstances our embrace might feel awkward to me, out of place and certainly out of character.

But in the Dog Chapel, I experience this holding of a complete stranger as a sort of communion—a sharing of something with another, something intimate and important. We come to this chapel—Tim, I, and so many others—to experience a communion of compassion and understanding, a communion that most often takes the form of words posted on walls. It's not the body of Christ or the cup of salvation that we share in this place. It's something less metaphorical, more earthly. But I have no doubt that on this afternoon in the Dog Chapel, the love of God and the fellowship of the Holy Spirit is very much with us.

WHEN I'M HOME in Medford I go to a different kind of church, a big, soaring structure in Harvard Yard, complete with choral music so beautiful I doubt that even the angels could improve upon it. Like the Dog Chapel, this church is meant to be a memorial—a memorial to Harvard's war dead. The names of those who lost their lives, the dates marking the boundaries of their existence, their University affiliation, and the wars in which they fought are neatly inscribed on stone tablets affixed to the sanctuary walls.

But I'm never particularly moved by reading those names, not the way I am in the Dog Chapel. A name etched into stone, the tablet cold to the touch and static in its placement, tells me nothing of real importance about the person memorialized there, and so provides me no means by which to emotionally connect. I experience the overall effect as cold and sterile, a memorial devoid of any remnant of humanity. The Dog Chapel, though, is alive and organic, the names on its walls handwritten on paper that can be removed, held, and replaced, the dogs memorialized there brought to vivid life through stories and photographs that allow me to know, to understand, to care.

Sitting in my pew every Sunday, surrounded by those stone tablets, I sometimes wonder what the Pusey Minister would do if he were to enter the sanctuary one morning and find flowers and notes attached to the stones beside some of the names, like at the Vietnam Memorial in Washington, D.C., or discover the celadon-colored walls covered with post-its and cards and letters from his congregation to their deceased loved ones. My guess is that, unlike Stephen Huneck, he'd have them removed as soon as possible and most certainly before Sunday morning's service.

I don't go to Memorial Church for the sermons. The reason I attend this church, music aside, is to be in the presence of the Reverend Dr. Dorothy Austin's prayers. Those prayers are a weekly salve, soothing the parts of my soul that feel tight and painful. And so it is now for me in the Dog Chapel, where the reverent words of kindred souls silently tend to and heal my broken and wounded parts. I experience in this place a true communion of the saints, human and canine, and it's this that both opens and transforms me.

I know that when Chispa dies, there'll be no flowers for her on the altar in the big church in Harvard Yard, no formal religious rite to commend her spirit into the hands of God. As a person of faith, I once experienced this as damaging and diminishing, but no longer. There will be a note written for her in my steady hand, left on a wall in the Dog Chapel with love, tears, and gratitude, and that will be more than enough.

SIXTEEN

THE MORNING AFTER my epiphany in the Dog Chapel, I sit on the chaise in the living room with Chispa while Marisel makes coffee. I hold Chispa's face between my hands and look deeply into her eyes, searching for some glimmer of recognition. But I see nothing in those cloudy brown eyes, nothing but fear and anxiety. There'll be no reconsidering my decision this time.

Marisel and I sit together at the kitchen table, coffee mugs in hand. I'm slow to wake, but as the caffeine enters my bloodstream and the last wisp of early-morning mental fog clears, I place my mug on the table and look at Marisel.

"We need to talk about Chispa."

She looks at me, one eyebrow raised.

"I'm not questioning our decision to put her down, just whether we want to have Maija come to the house and put her down here, or whether we should bring her to VESCONE. What do you think?"

When we put Laika down, we were grateful to be able to give her the gift of spending her last moments in the familiar comfort of her own home. But although I want the same for Chispa, I have reservations about it being the right way to go in this situation.

"I think Chispa would prefer to be at home, Pea."

"I do, too . . . It's just that I'm afraid things will go wrong . . ."

"What kind of things?"

"I don't know . . . I guess I wonder if because of the dementia, the process might be more complicated or something. I just want it all to be as easy as possible for her."

"Me, too."

"I'm planning to call Bari today to let her know we've decided it's time. I'll ask her what she thinks."

By the time I speak with Bari later in the day, I've thought through our options more fully and I'd much prefer that Chispa not have to make the trip to VESCONE. I still worry that the process may not go smoothly for her, though, and decide that I want Bari, who knows Chispa and her history inside out, to be the attending vet.

But when I ask Bari if she can put Chispa down at home, she explains that Massachusetts recently passed a law making it illegal for any vet without a mobile practice to perform in-home euthanasia. I'm outraged by this law, consider it unfair and absurd, but can't ask her to break it. Law aside, though, Bari thinks things may not go easily for Chispa and feels putting her down in the hospital will probably be best. Reluctantly, I agree.

I then share the process of how Marisel and I came to the decision to let Chispa go. I need Bari's approval, know I won't take the final step without it. She's in complete agreement that it's time.

"You've done everything you could possibly do for her, Gail. Most people would've given up a long time ago."

I pause for a moment to let her words sink in. I'm relieved by the first part of what she says, but the second part is, to my mind, open to multiple interpretations."

"I know we're making the right decision, but it's still so hard to let her go."

"I know. It's hard for me, too. I'm going to miss her. I've been her vet for pretty much her entire life."

That Bari cares about my dog enough to miss her means a lot to me, and I try not to think about the fact that when I lose Chispa I'll also lose Bari. VESCONE is an emergency and specialty center only, and Chula has no chronic illnesses, no need for the ongoing care of a highly trained internal medicine specialist. It's too much loss for me to process at one time, and I shut down emotionally, focusing my conversation with Bari on details, specifics—the kinds of tangible things my mind is able to grasp.

"We'd like to set up the appointment in the next few days."

In spite of all I know and believe with certainty about my dog's state of being, in spite of even myself, I want just a little more time with her. The firmly rooted habits of wanting and grasping, of holding on to love and life, are not easily pulled from their psychic soil and discarded.

"Okay. How about Thursday morning at eleven?"

"That's fine."

But, of course, it's not.

There's something indescribably heartbreaking and even slightly macabre about choosing the day and time my dog will die. In my mind I begin a mental countdown of the remaining hours of her life. I know that from this moment forward, when I look at her I'll see a shadowy specter, the ghost of the moment when I'll give her life over, first to Bari and then to God. It's almost unbearable to contemplate, almost enough to make me tell Bari no, I've changed my mind. Almost.

Bari and I exchange a few more words, but they slip from my memory once spoken. Chispa, Marisel, and I will arrive at VESCONE in three more days, at eleven in the morning. That's the limit of the information my brain can take in. I hang up the phone and sit alone in my office at work, staring numbly out the window, seeing nothing.

It's difficult to concentrate on my students' need to find a summer internship or post-graduation job, more difficult yet to appreciate their angst and sense of urgency relative to their career plans or lack thereof. I don't care about their turmoil, their confusion, their need for a letter explaining the school's policy on academic credit for internships. Why do they bother me with these things? Don't they know my dog will be dead in three days? I yearn to walk out of my office, to be home with Marisel, the one person I don't need to explain myself to, don't need to submerge my emotions around. When five o'clock finally arrives, it seems one of the greatest blessings of my life.

Later that evening, I reiterate the details of my conversation with Bari to Marisel—the appointment I've made, the idiotic euthanasia law. Chispa walks aimlessly through the first-floor rooms as I speak, completing lap after lap. The words that pass between me and Marisel, well outside the range of a dog's limited vocabulary of human words, are nothing but meaningless sounds to Chispa. I wish she'd stop her pacing, jump up on the chaise beside me and fall into the deep, undisturbed peace of sleep, but it's a while before her wandering tires her sufficiently for that relief.

"What do you think? Do you agree with Bari about bringing Chispa to VESCONE?"

"I guess so, Pea. I wish she could be at home instead, but I think we should go with what Bari thinks is best."

So this is what the last five months of our dog's life has finally come to—a date and time set to release her from her life with us into eternal freedom from ailments of mind and body. The letting go is, I suppose, the price we tacitly agreed to pay for the gift of Chispa's life, for the privilege of guardianship, but now that the time has come to settle our debt, we don't do so gladly.

Chispa lies beside me on the chaise now, sound asleep, her closed eyes hiding all traces of the emptiness that resides within them. It's in sleep that I miss her most. I stare at the slow rise and fall of her rib cage, mesmerized as always by the utter miracle of it. In a little more than two days her chest will no longer rise, no longer fall. She will be gone. I'm overcome by the now familiar urge to lean over and hold her as tightly as I can, for as long as I can. But I resist, choose instead to let her sleep.

The following days pass in that odd and contradictory way that typifies a death watch. Time goes by too quickly, and yet so slowly. I'm simultaneously aware of nothing and everything—tuned in to every detail of Chispa's face and body and actions, focused on everything that's been a part of her life, of the life she's shared with Marisel and me. The rest of the details of my life, of the world itself, pass by unnoticed. Are bills past due? Have we paid the mortgage? I have no idea. Those things don't concern me. All that matters to me is that the world as I've come to know it over the past fourteen years, the world that still includes Chispa, will be over in two days. Until then, I will hold onto every second, minute, hour, and day of it, and burn them into my brain.

I think back to the very beginning, to the moment I first saw Chispa on that beach in Vieques, to the moment I looked into her eyes while she lay stretched on the villa floor watching me, the exact moment I knew she belonged with me. I recall the months and years of her life, all that's passed since then. Her muzzle is gray now, her joints stiff and achy, her gait slower. She no longer runs. Yet even as these facts of her physical aging stare brazenly back at me when I look at her, I still see her as vibrant, loving, happy, and endlessly curious about everything that comprises her small corner of the world.

The dog pacing through the house or vocalizing anxiously looks like Chispa, yes. But that dog isn't Chispa, not the real Chispa. The real Chispa is the dog I see in my mind's eye now and will always see, the dog whose soul I hope to release to joy and peace, as she once released mine.

And then, suddenly, it's Thursday morning. I've been expecting its arrival, have spent the past days preparing for it. Still, inexplicably, I'm surprised to find it actually here. I'm seized by a momentary panic, a regression. Are we really doing the right thing? Before my mind can grab onto this question and run off with it in a thousand different and destructive directions, a firm voice from somewhere within me utters a simple word intended for my brain: *Stop.* And, incredibly, it does—but not before uttering its own, even simpler word: *Yes.*

I get out of bed and go downstairs. Marisel's already up, making coffee. The normalcy of it all belies the events of the day, the grief that will wash over me like a landslide in the next few hours, burying me beneath suffocating layers of complicated emotions. I've been in a state of anticipatory grief for days now, ever since my final decision in the Dog Chapel. But I know from past experience that no period of anticipatory grief will ever be long enough to alleviate the real thing. I'm sliding slowly but headlong into Grief, and nothing can change that.

It's an incongruously beautiful day, and I open the sliders to let the dogs out into the back yard. I stand on the deck, steam rising from my coffee cup, and watch them, their contrasting ways of being, perhaps now more a function of aging than of innate personality. Chispa walks along slowly until she does her business, repeating the same process several times, while Chula runs in circles that get smaller and tighter with each revolution, sniffing the ground until she finds just the right place to pee.

My dogs. Soon there will be just one.

I can't bring myself to call them inside. I want Chispa to lie down on the grass near the shed, to feel the warmth of the early morning sun on her body for as long as she pleases. Tomorrow's sun will rise and warm without her. Marisel comes out onto the deck with me and we both lean over the railing, watching Chispa standing contentedly in a patch of sunlight.

"How can we take this away from her?" I ask.

"The disease is taking it away from her, not us."

I'm grateful for this reframing and squeeze her hand tightly.

In a little less than two hours, it will be time to leave. I bring the dogs back inside and feed them. I can't manage to eat anything more substantial than a protein shake, and even that doesn't go down easily. Feeling as if each swallow might spontaneously eject itself back from where it came, I bring the nearly full glass upstairs and leave it on the bedside table while I take a shower.

As the hot water flows over my body, I feel the knots in my upper back loosen just enough to release my shoulders to their normal resting place. I ask myself what now, what to do until we leave. Do we simply sit together? Is there anything Chispa might like to do one last time, anything she might like to see or smell? I've done things this way only once, with our cat Lucy. I wasn't skilled at it then, and feel even less skilled at it now.

I remain in the shower, hoping for a baptism of sorts, that I might be born again into new life—a life in which I know how to meet death, am not afraid to look it in the face, can cherish, rather than simply intellectually acknowledge, its possibilities for growth and insight. But after another five minutes in the shower I give up, accept that today is not the day on which I'll be reborn. I turn off the water, get dressed, and go downstairs. There's nothing to do now except wait.

Our cat Mandu, always sensitive to both human and animal vibes in our home, seems to know there's something different about this morning. Quietly, slowly, he approaches Chispa, who's lying on her orthopedic bed in the living room vocalizing. Mandu usually runs off at the sound of Chispa's agitated barking, perhaps frightened by the anxiety it conveys to him. But this morning he gathers his courage and stands beside her. He sniffs her body, and rubs his head quickly on her side, a tiny and loving head butt. Then he races off, across the room and up the stairs to the safety of his favorite chair in the study. I understand that he has just said good-bye.

And then it's Chula's turn. She and Chispa lie together on the living room rug, face to face. Chula leans forward and licks Chispa's muzzle, over and over again, as if she knows this will be her last chance to express her love and gratitude for the old dog who so easily accepted her into the pack. Chispa licks Chula's face, too, a series of tender dog kisses that seem both a thank you and a good-bye. I leave the room and go upstairs, not wanting to cry in their presence.

Finally, it's time to leave. I slip Chispa's rainbow harness over her head, the same harness we put on her when we brought her home from Vieques all those years ago. Marisel clips a leash onto the d-ring, and we stand together in the tiny foyer, the three of us, for one last time. We stand like this for no more than a few seconds, seconds that encapsulate the entirety of what it means to love a dog. Then we walk out of the house and down the front steps, Chispa never once turning to look back. As I help her into the back seat of my car, I'm grateful for this one small mercy.

SEVENTEEN

THERE'S NOT MUCH to say, and Marisel and I exchange minimal words on the drive to VESCONE. Chispa's vocalization, though, has reached fever pitch, spurred by the anxiety of being in the car. She used to love to ride, but no longer. Marisel sits in the back seat with her, trying to comfort her. But she's beyond comfort and continues her frantic barking for the duration of the trip.

Unsettled by the level of noise in the car, distracted by the enormous effort of trying to hold my emotions together, I almost drive right by the parking lot. My quick, sharp turn to avoid missing the entrance startles my back-seat passengers.

"Pea, what the hell . . ."

"Sorry. I almost missed it."

Even Chispa is momentarily shocked into silence. But as soon as I park the car and turn off the ignition, her vocalizing resumes.

"Maybe we should walk her for a few minutes before we go inside," I suggest.

Marisel agrees, and I lead Chispa in the direction of the path at the end of the parking lot. The path is short and wooded, carpeted in pine needles, and leads to a shaded picnic area. I've always thought this an odd place for a picnic table, as there's clearly a subset of dog owners for whom the purpose of those little plastic bags in the box near the path's entrance remains a mystery.

Still, the picnic table provides a comfortable place to sit, and I settle myself on one of its benches while Chispa shuffles around, sniffing the scents other dogs have left behind. I can't help but wonder what information she finds in those scents. Or are they meaningless now, the urge to smell them nothing more than a habit, an instinct?

The trees surrounding the path and picnic table muffle the sounds of the busy road in front of VESCONE, and as the minutes pass I become acutely aware of the sound of birds. I listen carefully, paying attention to the different notes and nuances of the various songs. Something about these bird songs, about the joy of new life on a sunny morning in May, juxtaposed with death, is familiar to me. I can't shake the feeling of déjà vu, and eventually make the connection. I sat in much the same way on a bright spring morning a little over a decade ago, in the pew of a small Episcopal church on the day of my grandmother's funeral service, listening to the birds singing.

New life, in all its forms.

It's a while before I realize that my dog will die ten years to the very day after my grandmother, who, like Chispa, spent the last year of her life tangled in dementia.

Eventually Chispa tires of her olfactory exploration, and Marisel and I look at each other. It's time to go inside.

"C'mon, good girl. Let's go."

We all turn around and head back down the path, away from the shade of the trees and the singing of the birds and the lingering smell of un-scooped poop. The path is a bit too narrow for three, so Marisel walks up ahead. Chispa plods along behind her, just a short bit ahead of me. As soon as we reach the parking lot and VESCONE comes into view, Chispa begins vocalizing. For a quick moment, panic overtakes me— does she know why we've brought her here? Is that why she's barking so loudly and frantically? It's not too late to go inside and tell Bari we've changed our minds, not too late to put Chispa back in the car and drive home.

Somehow, I'm able to talk myself down. This is just what she does now, I remind myself silently, the tone of my internal voice so calm and rational, so unlike my usual voice in times of crisis, that it seems to come from someone else. It doesn't matter where she is or what she's doing. She's in a nearly constant state of anxiety, and this is how she expresses it. It has nothing to do with where we're going, what will happen. She doesn't have the ability to sense those kinds of things, not anymore.

We walk through the set of automatic doors leading into VESCONE's lobby, Chispa barking so loudly that the receptionist and I can barely carry on a conversation. The young woman knows Chispa well, has seen her in much better times. She looks at me with kindness and compassion, a look that has the tendency to make me fall apart. I tear up but otherwise manage to maintain my composure. She tells me Bari will be with us shortly, and Marisel and I take a seat in the far end of the lobby with Chispa.

It's soon apparent that waiting inside isn't an option. Chispa's barking continues unabated, perhaps the loudest it's ever been. I glance over at the receptionist as she struggles to hear the person on the other end of the telephone.

"We need to take Chispa outside," I tell Marisel.

She nods and takes Chispa's leash from me, and the two of them disappear through the automatic doors. The silence they leave behind is deafening.

I let the receptionist know where we'll be, then go outside to wait with Marisel and Chispa. I find myself hoping for some delay, some emergency case for Bari to deal with before it's Chispa's turn. And maybe there really is an emergency—the wait does seem longer than usual. For once, I don't care about waiting. I'm not irritated by the waste of time. I'm simply grateful for whatever extra moments I'm given with my dog.

It's sunny and very warm outside, the way the three of us prefer our weather. Not too long ago, Chispa would have considered a day like this perfect for asphalt-lying, an island habit she never outgrew and one I never quite understood. I hope now that she might lie down on the very warm cement here, on this secluded little walkway right alongside the building, and sleep for a bit. But she doesn't. Her anxiety seems to have overtaken her, and she's unable to do anything but bark and, to the extent her leash will allow, pace.

My bones greedily suck up the rays of the mid-spring sun, spreading a current of warmth throughout my body. It calms me, but only slightly. Chispa's barking has taken on an odd, hollow tone, and my heart breaks at the sound of it. There's something about those barks that seems so ancient, and so very lonely. And suddenly, I want someone to walk out of that glass hospital door, *now*, and tell us Bari's ready for Chispa. I want my sweet, smart, quirky, loved-beyond-words dog to be at peace.

It's a few more minutes, but finally Amy, Bari's technician, comes out to get us. She brings us through a side door I've never paid much attention to, a door that leads to the room I call the grief cocoon, but which I'm sure the VESCONE staff calls by another name. She leaves us in the room for a brief time, and then returns with Bari. Bari sits on the floor next to Chispa, stroking her head, hoping to calm the barking. But there's no calming Chispa.

"Is this pretty much what she's been like recently, or is this a function of her being here?"

"This is pretty much what she's like now."

In the long pause that follows, each of us looks at Chispa, wishing things were different.

"You're doing the right thing."

Bari's confirmation is, to me, a benediction.

"I know . . . but it's still so hard."

Those last few words have a strange choked sound, as if first squeezed and then propelled through the vocal cords of one who simultaneously doesn't want to speak them and can't speak them fast enough. I fight to hold my emotions together, wanting to provide Chispa with the calm environment the Buddhists believe is most conducive to the soul's peaceful passage out of this life. I'll cry, but not now.

Bari explains how things will go.

"She's obviously very agitated, so I'm going to give her a tranquilizer before I administer the euthanasia medication. I want to make sure the process goes smoothly for her. After she gets the tranquilizer I'll bring her back here, and you can take as much time as you need with her."

"Can we put her down in here instead of in an exam room?" I ask. The room, with its thick rug, sofa, chair, and prints on the walls, seems more like home.

"Of course."

Bari gets up from the floor and takes Chispa's leash. "C'mon, Chi, let's go. We'll be right back."

Chispa walks with Bari and Amy out of the room and down the hall that leads to the place generally referred to as "out back"," a place I've never seen but imagine to be a large medical area of some sort. I can hear Chispa barking as they make their way to wherever it is they're going. The extra tranquilizer is a godsend. I can't imagine her dying with such anxiety.

Chispa returns shortly and I'm surprised to find her still barking.

"She'll be much calmer in a few minutes," Bari tells us. "With her being so agitated, it may take the tranquilizer a little longer to have an effect."

That makes sense.

"Take as much time as you need with her, and when you're ready just let us know."

And then Marisel and I are left alone to say our good-byes to Chispa.

But it's not at all as we'd expected, certainly not at all what we'd hoped for. Rather than being calm, Chispa seems even more anxious, vocalizing frantically. We try to hold her, try to get her to lie down on the blanket Amy brought in for her, but she won't have any of it. This is not how we want to say good-bye to her, not how we want her to die.

Bari appears at the door within minutes, her eyes filled with concern for Chispa, and for Marisel and me as well.

"I can't let this go on. I can give her a second dose, but once I do that, there's no turning back."

"We just want her to be able to die peacefully."

"Okay."

Bari leaves and quickly returns with the injection. She kneels on the floor beside my suffering dog, leans over her with a syringe, and depresses the plunger. Almost immediately after the fluid disappears into Chispa's skin, the room is filled with a silence so abrupt, so unexpected, that I experience a momentary sense of disequilibrium.

Marisel and I sit on the floor beside Chispa, speaking softly, telling her over and over again how much we love her, how graced our lives have been by her. I thank her for hauling me from the depths of grief after Comet died, for restoring me to myself bit by piece. Leaning closer, I bury my face in her fur, inhale that odd Fritos scent of her. It's a smell that will always, in my mind, belong to her. Sorry, Frito-Lay.

We say everything that needs saying in less than a minute. She's more than halfway gone now, and we don't want to keep her soul from its destination any longer. I tell Bari we're ready.

"Okay. It'll be easy now, I promise."

In the last few seconds before the final injection stops Chispa's heart, Marisel and I lean over our old girl, arms around her still body, wanting our hands and voices to be the final things to usher her from this world.

"'Bye, sweetheart. Go find Tomas and Laika . . . They're waiting for you."

My whispered words still hang in the air as Bari gently places the stethoscope against Chispa's heart, then looks up at us and nods her head.

"She's gone."

The Word of Dog
FRIEND

"You were beautiful, intelligent, and very wise. I'll miss you. Your buddy, Red."

"Dear Belle-Belle—You were a great friend to me. I love you and I'll see you on the other side."

"To Hannah—A friend that gave me a sense of direction. Always in my heart. Wait for me."

"Griffey—Best dog I could ask for. Thanks for everything you did for me. I wish you didn't pass so suddenly and at such a young age. You had so much more to offer to the world. You were my best friend and most loyal companion. Rest in doggy heaven, pal."

"Mojo, Never again could we have a dog as special as you. You were my best friend and always will be. I will always love you no matter what happens I will always love you. R.I.P. Mojo. Life isn't the same without you."

"Destiny, Truffles and Quincy—I know you are all having fun together, and are best friends, up in dog heaven. You brought me much joy in my life. I love and miss all of you."

"For my puppy, my dog "LUCKY"—Miss you sprawled on the bathroom floor. Miss you sitting on the porch on a summer nite. Sleep well, my friend, till we meet again."

"Harry was a 'class act'…and a devoted friend and companion for all his years on this planet. He will be terribly missed, and we are comforted to know he is with Chris now, waiting for Jen and Barkley to join him."

"Bear—Best Dog Ever! We will love you and miss you always. Rest easy, our faithful friend. Catch it in the air!!"

EIGHTEEN

IN THE DAYS after Chispa's death, I'm stalked incessantly by the quiet that pervades every space in which she once existed. It follows me everywhere, this deep quiet. It rides in the car with me, an uninvited passenger making its presence known even over the strains of Handel or Bach. It accompanies me as I move through the house, managing to be heard over the running water when I stand in the shower. It's odd, this silence. Only a month ago I craved it, yearned for it, my nerves frayed as they were from the constant barking. And now that I have it I want it gone, want not to be reminded of the profound absence held within every moment of that silence, the absence that is the source of my grief.

I miss her. I don't regret our decision to let her go, but lack of regret doesn't mitigate grief. I grieve for the loss of the dog she was before CDS and spend hours each day visiting that dog in my mind's eye, the many moments of her happy life with us. That dog had to have known how intensely she was loved.

But what of the dog she became, the dog whose life was stolen from her in so many ways by a disease that spares neither human nor animal? What, if anything, did this dog know? I wait for her to visit me in my dreams, hoping for a sign that she's found her way to new life.

I find the existence and differing manifestations of the ways in which my animals have communicated with me shortly after dying fascinating. Not too long after Laika's death, Marisel pulled into our gravel driveway in New Hampshire. As she parked the car and turned off the ignition, she heard Laika's bark—just one bark, but a bark so distinctive there was no mistaking it, a bark that sounded like the word "alright" but with an "r" preceding the first syllable and the "l" sound more like a "w." For several nights after Nike died, I lay awake in the darkness listening to the sound of her breathing, its audible rasp coming from the area of the bedroom where she always slept. Comet came to me in an exuberant dream, running like the wind in a wide open space, and Pez with a gentle head butt to the small of my back as I sat on my heels dusting the baseboards in the master bathroom. I recognize and understand each of these fleeting experiences for what I believe them to be—a parting gift from the dead to the living, a gift of love and healing.

I know the sign from Chispa will eventually appear, but I need it now. I wait for days, my grief intensifying, and then, nearly a week after Chispa dies, the sign comes. Marisel and I sit at the kitchen table drinking espresso in a deep and heavy silence, both of us lost in private grief, until the silence is unexpectedly broken by the clear sound of a bell. The ring is brief and not particularly loud, as if a person or animal had just barely brushed by the bell in passing. The only bell we have in the house is a sleigh bell, hanging on a red cord from the knob of the door leading to the basement. We're sitting less than five feet from the bell. It would be difficult to mistake its ringing for something else.

"Did you hear that?"

Marisel nods.

"What did you hear?" I need to be sure.

"A bell."

Chula and Mandu are elsewhere, and the early morning air is still too chilly for open windows. But the bell clearly rang; we both heard it. We look at each other now and smile.

"I think Chispa's trying to tell us she's alright, Pea."

And with the sound of that bell, my stalker departs.

NINETEEN

ON MY WAY to VESCONE to pick up Chispa's ashes, I experience a growing sense of excitement and anticipation, as if I'm going to see her again. The sensation is simultaneously odd and familiar—odd in that it makes no sense, familiar in that there's the strong sense of déjà vu, as if I'm simply driving to the hospital to pick her up, and will walk out with her, put her in the car, and drive her home, as I've done every time but the last. And that's exactly the way it will be—except that instead of holding onto Chispa's leash, I'll be holding a small cardboard box containing an even smaller wooden box, the bits of bone and ashes secured within it all I have left of Chispa's physical being. Still, in whatever form, my beloved dog will be home.

We won't bury the ashes. We refuse to commit them to the ground that freezes in winter, to a patch of earth that belongs to us only for the time we remain in our house. And scattering them doesn't feel permanent enough to me. Instead, Chispa's ashes will join the others, urns placed on various shelves and tables in our warm and sunny study, hers adding yet another dimension to the visual representation of our aggregate loss.

When I arrive home, Marisel and I open the cardboard box and remove Chispa's urn. It's a beautiful cherry wood, heavier than I expect. The urn is different from any of the others, with a decorative brass clasp on the front held together by a small gold-plated padlock. Attached to the padlock by a miniature key ring are two tiny keys. Marisel looks at me.

"Should we open it?"

I struggle to answer. There's a part of me that wants to hold those bones and ashes against my heart, as if by doing so Chispa might somehow be magically resurrected, right here in our living room. But there's another part of me that doesn't want to see what's in the box, that doesn't have the emotional fortitude to stare down the remnants of death in that way. *Remember that thou art dust, and to dust thou shalt return.* I accept both the truth and inevitability of this, but prefer to remember my dog not as dust but as a living being made of flesh and blood and fur.

"No."

"I want to see what the ashes look like."

She's curious in that way, much more pragmatic than I about both life and death.

"If you want to open it, go ahead. But don't do it while I'm still here."

I leave the urn with her and go upstairs into the library. The day's light is beginning its fade, the first streaks of pink forming in the sky to the west. I sit in my great-grandfather's rocking chair and push myself slowly back and forth, random images from my life with Chispa appearing in my mind's eye.

I see her in New Hampshire, walking up a wooded path ahead of me. She stops, turning her head over her shoulder to look at me, making sure I haven't disappeared, haven't left her behind. There she is in the driveway in Chelsea, lying in the sun on the roof of my car. Now she's stretched out beside my beach chair on the rocky sand by the stream up at Zealand, muzzle resting on her front paws, watching Laika wade into the icy water. I see her with Tomas, settled at his feet under the grape arbor heavy with late summer's purple bounty. I see myself noticing her for the first time on the beach in Vieques, feel my chest tighten now just as it had back then. My wonderful, glorious girl . . . God, how I miss her.

I never ask Marisel if she opened the urn.

TWENTY

ON THE MIDDLE day of one of the most beautiful Memorial Day weekends in recent memory, Marisel and I attend Stephen Huneck's memorial service on Dog Mountain. Dogs have also been invited to attend, and we've brought Chula with us. As we make our way across the yard, colorful paper prayer flags strung across the white picket fences flutter, as if even the inanimate has been given life on this day.

Dogs are everywhere, chasing each other up and down the hillside, trotting in and out of the chapel, jumping with abandon into the pond. If one were to randomly happen across the Dog Chapel on this early Sunday afternoon, it would be nearly impossible to imagine that within an hour, everyone will be seated in rows of chairs set up on the hillside, dogs lying quietly beside their people, to remember the man who loved this place into existence. I smile, thinking how much Stephen would enjoy the cacophony of barking, splashing, and laughter. If he could have scripted his own memorial service, I imagine this is exactly what he would've had in mind.

It's a strange feeling, being here under these circumstances. Everything about my experience of this place has become a reverse image of itself. The dogs that capture my attention today are not the dogs on the walls of the chapel but the dogs on the hillsides and in the water, the dogs stealing hot dogs and burgers from people silly enough to leave their plates on the ground—living, breathing, three-dimensional dogs reminding me with every fiber of their beings that life is meant to be lived with joy. I know Stephen knew this, because that message radiates through every element of his work. Yet somehow, in the grip of whatever demons, it was forgotten.

Despite having not known Stephen, I can't imagine being anywhere else today. I need to be here on Dog Mountain, in the company of my tribe, to say both thank you and good-bye to the man whose life and work shone such a light for so many. Along with almost everyone else who's come to remember Stephen and celebrate his life, Marisel and I want to spend some quiet time before the service in the Dog Chapel. We enter the chapel, hoping to feel Stephen's presence there.

With the obvious exception of the notes on its walls, everything that constitutes the Dog Chapel has at one time rested in Stephen's hands—has been held, turned, shaped, cut, polished, perfected by him. I don't believe it's possible for an artist to create a work of this magnitude without permanently infusing it with a profound element of self, and I envision his spirit being drawn back to this place where so much of who he was has been left behind.

For the first time, it occurs to me that perhaps what I've experienced as divine energy during my visits to the chapel over these past few years has instead been the loving life force Stephen breathed into every piece of its wood and glass. But before this thought has been fully processed, I understand that it doesn't matter—in so many ways, it's all the same.

Marisel and I walk up the chapel's granite steps with Chula, and once inside I immediately notice something different. The notes and photos on the left wall of the vestibule have been removed, the space turned into a memorial for Stephen. We walk over to the wall and slowly travel from one end to the other, reading the notes left behind, smiling at the many pictures chronicling Stephen's life with Gwen and their various dogs.

In photo after photo, I search his face for some indication of the torment that led him to pull that trigger, to end his life in an instant, but see none. Can despair that dark even be captured in a photograph? I have no idea, no personal frame of reference from which to consider the question. All I know of what's transpired is that I feel the loss of this man I never knew down to the bone.

I want to add my own public note of thanks to Stephen's wall, and select a hot pink post-it from the pile on the familiar wooden table. I choose my words carefully, as if he might one day read them. I want him to know how much I love the Dog Chapel, the extent to which what lies within it has transformed me. We've arrived well ahead of the main crowd, and there's plenty of open space on the wall to attach my note. I choose a place just below a photo of Stephen and his adored black Lab, Sally.

We then enter the sanctuary, and sit in our pew to pray for Stephen and for the family and friends he's left behind. I pray that he will find, in the everlasting company of a loving God, the peace that eluded him in life. And I pray that those he loved will eventually find their own peace.

Marisel is still deep in prayer. I leave her in the pew with Chula and begin a slow, reverent walk around the Dog Chapel.

I notice that one of Stephen's works has been placed in an upright position on the floor near the chapel's west wall. The print, a reproduction of the original, is entitled "It Wouldn't be Heaven Without Dogs." Stephen's body of work depicts many images of his belief in a happy afterlife for pets, including dogs and cats with angel wings flying upward toward heaven, and a dog holding a brown shoe in her mouth, the print's caption reading "Dogs Have a Soul." The print on the floor of the Dog Chapel, though, is much more intricate—a detailed depiction of heaven as only an animal lover could imagine it.

In Stephen's vision of heaven, the entrance is a gold picket fence floating on a series of white fluffy clouds, the sections of the fence separated by red brick pillars. Just in case those who've arrived at the gate are unsure of where they are, the word "Heaven" is spelled out in large black letters across a golden arch supported by the two center pillars. Beneath the "Heaven" sign is a gold arched doorway with the words "Good People" written on it, and on either side of that doorway are two smaller but otherwise identical doorways, one bearing the words "Good Dogs," and the smallest one inscribed with the words "Good Cats."

A female angel with long dark hair and golden wings flies along over the "Heaven" arch. A black Lab floats in front of her with his own set of gold wings, his red leash held in the angel's hand. To the right of the "Heaven" arch, a golden retriever and a black-and-white cat fly through the sky together, both, of course, with beautiful golden wings. All the angels—the woman, the dogs, and particularly the cat—look happy.

As I stare at the print, mesmerized, I envision Stephen in a place exactly like the one he's created on wood and paper: A heaven populated by good people, good dogs, and good cats, surrounded by his own deceased pets and by all the animals memorialized in the Dog Chapel. The vision in my head seems so right, and makes me smile. Marisel joins me in front of the print, and we both agree that it's an almost perfect representation of our own interpretation of heaven.

AT SLIGHTLY PAST the appointed time, with people seated in chairs and dogs stretched out on the grass, Stephen's service begins. His death and the reasons for it are discussed openly, shedding light on what was, for so many, incomprehensible. There are loving testimonials from his family, his employees, and his friends. But the words that affect me most come from a woman who recounts a story of having met Stephen many years ago in a shop where some of his prints were for sale.

She fell in love with one particular print hanging in the shop, she explains, but was very poor back then. She spent hours looking at it, loving it, wanting it, but knew she couldn't afford it. She walked away several times, focusing on other items in the shop, but always returned to stand before the print and stare, unable to purchase it, unable not to. Eventually a man in the store struck up a conversation with her about the print, and she confessed that she adored the work and would love to buy it, but that it was well beyond her means. As it turned out, the man was Stephen Huneck, the artist whose work she'd spent the past few hours admiring.

"He arranged for me to put ten dollars down, take the print home with me, and make monthly payments on it. I paid ten dollars every month for years, but I eventually paid it off. He didn't even know me, but he wanted me to have the print because I loved it, and he trusted that I'd make the payments. I've never forgotten that. That's the kind of person Stephen was."

Another woman rises to speak and offers a vision of hope for us all.

"I believe there's a special area in heaven for dogs and that Stephen is there, watching them all crossing over the Rainbow Bridge, taking care of them and baking dog biscuits for them."

May it be so, I pray silently. May it be so.

The testimonials ended, we leave our seats and reassemble near the entrance to the gallery. From here the minister and Gwen lead us up the dirt road to the very top of Dog Mountain. Marisel, Chula, and I have fallen behind the larger group, and by the time we arrive at the clearing on the top of the hill the minister has already begun to speak. I wonder what the next segment of this most untraditional memorial service will consist of, whether the minister will now read, at least in part, the liturgy for the dead. But no—those of us gathered on the highest point on Dog Mountain hear an altogether different sort of liturgy.

Over the years Stephen had written a series of *New York Times* best-selling books featuring his black Lab Sally as the protagonist. But there was one Sally manuscript that had yet to be published at the time of his death: *Sally Goes to Heaven*. Now, as the minister stands beneath the super-sized carving of the iconic winged dog that graces the peak of Dog Mountain, it's the words of Stephen's unpublished manuscript—a completely revised and re-imagined liturgy of the dead—that he reads.

In the story, Sally wakes up one morning feeling tired and achy, and not very hungry. She walks around her home, and then lies down to take a nap. When she wakes up she finds herself in another place—a place where all her pains are gone and there are unlimited amounts of all her favorite things.

In this new place, there are ice cream stands on every corner, meatballs hanging from trees, lots of other dogs to play with, no animal shelters, and—perhaps most exciting of all—an enormous pile of dirty socks. Whenever she thinks about how much she'd like to have her belly rubbed, children appear and fulfill her wish in unlimited quantities. There's a big window where Sally can look in on her family, and she wishes she could tell them she's happy and free from pain. She hopes they'll adopt another dog, and that they won't be sad for too long.

As I listen to Stephen's wonderful vision of a dog's heaven, I find myself alternating between tears and laughter. The idea of Chispa looking through a window at us, checking up on us to see how we're doing, makes me cry. Somehow, the thought of her seeing us but not being seen in return triggers an intense and painful sense of loneliness, and I wonder if this is what she feels when she peeks down at us through that window. But the image of her turning every corner and finding her favorite things makes me smile, and as I visualize in greater detail exactly what heaven for Chispa might look like, I begin to laugh.

I see her now, free from arthritis and dementia, running with Laika or sitting quietly in the company of Lucy, Martina, and Pez. I see her greeting Tomas, and meeting Comet and Nike for the first time. In Chispa's heaven, I'm sure there are dog biscuit dispensers every few feet. The sun shines each day so she can lie outside baking in it, preferably on a patch of asphalt, and no one throws salt on the roads in winter because winter doesn't exist. Every night someone cooks a barbecue for her, and whenever she wants to take a nap there's someone she loves to cover her with a blanket.

The minister finishes reading and leads us, Stephen's congregation, in prayer. At the conclusion of the prayers, Gwen Huneck, holding a small box, makes her way to where the minister stands. He explains that in the box are butterflies, which will be released to mark the closing of the service. And then, with Gwen holding the box, the lid is lifted, releasing the black-and-orange butterflies to the freedom of Dog Mountain. We watch in silence, not wanting the service to end, not wanting the tribe to scatter. But eventually the silence is broken, and we begin the walk back down the steep dirt road toward the gallery.

As we walk slowly away from the top of Dog Mountain, I notice a few of the butterflies on the long blades of grass in the field along the road. Their wings quiver almost imperceptibly as they balance on the narrow surface of the grass, becoming one with the blade they've alighted on, moving and bending along with their temporary landing spot as each gust of breeze shifts it back and forth. Escaping the confinement of the box the butterflies seem reborn, filled with a new energy that leads them to seek not the security of a thick, stable tree branch but the vicissitudes of a tiny blade of grass.

We walk a bit farther down the road before I see it, the sign that Stephen is indeed with us. I look to my right, at another carving of the winged dog set just off the road, and there it is—a butterfly perched delicately on the dog's face. To me, the sign couldn't possibly be any clearer. I grab my camera to record the image, but in the few seconds it takes me to remove the camera from its case, the butterfly is gone.

I later discover that at least one other person saw what I saw halfway between the top of Dog Mountain and the Dog Chapel. The next time Marisel looks at the Dog Mountain Facebook page, a picture of the dog and butterfly is posted. I can't imagine how anyone looking at that photograph or seeing the image in person could understand it to be anything other than Stephen's way of letting us know that he's well, and at peace. I add this incident to the list of minor miracles I've experienced in and around the Dog Chapel.

I want a remembrance of this day, something other than photographs. I want something solid, something once held in Stephen's hands, infused with his creativity and loving spirit.

"Let's go look around in the gallery for a few minutes," I suggest.

Chula trots confidently up the gallery steps beside us, as if walking into a space filled with beautiful artwork is an everyday occurrence for her. While Marisel heads over to the water cooler with Chula, I move into the larger section of the gallery. I wander from one area to another, searching for just the right piece of art, one that will remind me of this day and of the human spirit's ability to create joy from even the most unimaginable grief. It's not long before I find it—a smaller version of the winged dog, this one in the image of a Dalmatian. I pick the carving up off the shelf, feeling the substantial weight of it in my hands, and begin walking toward the register.

I see Marisel and Chula heading in my direction, and I hold out the carving.

"I'm going to buy this."

Marisel takes the winged dog from me, and turns it in every direction, noticing every detail of it, before handing it back.

"It's beautiful. I love it."

I bring my winged Dalmation to the register and watch as the young woman who takes my payment carefully and lovingly wraps the carving in paper and places it gently in a sturdy paper bag, which I then give to Marisel.

"Hold this for me, okay? I want to go back to the Dog Chapel for a little bit. I won't be long."

"Sure. I'll probably just sit outside with Chula and wait for you."

I kiss them both, then walk out the gallery door and over to the Dog Chapel.

TWENTY-ONE

ENTERING THE DOG Chapel, I find myself in the company of several people and their dogs. We smile at each other, and I feel grateful for the presence of others in this place I usually prefer to visit alone. I walk over to the wooden table and select a pastel pink post-it pad, then rummage in my bag for a pen. There are pens scattered on the table, but for this note, I want to use my own.

I stand there for what seems just short of an eternity, pen in hand, elbows on the table, staring at the wall of notes and photographs in front of me. I don't seem to be able to find the right words to compose my remembrance for Laika and Chispa, the magical combination of letters and punctuation marks that will express the totality of my love for them and still fit on a post-it.

But this is the Dog Chapel, and I trust that the words will eventually come. And, after a time, they do.

"To our beloved dogs Laika and Chispa: We'll always remember the times we brought you to this blessed place. We miss you both so much, and see you everywhere we look. We grieve your loss, but also are filled with joyful gratitude for the gift to us that was your lives. We'll see you again. Your loving Moms."

I pick up a pushpin from the basket on the table and walk into the sanctuary. In all the years I've been visiting the Dog Chapel, Stephen never removed any of the remembrances posted on the walls, and now there are so many it would require days to read them all. It takes me a while, but I eventually manage to find a tiny open space for my remembrance on one of the rear walls. I push the pin into the wall through what feels like several layers of post-its and paper, then take a step back and read my remembrance once again. There's something so final about those words staring back at me in my own hand. Laika and Chispa are gone—there's a remembrance in the Dog Chapel that testifies to it.

Out of what I imagine to be force of habit, I begin to read some of the notes posted near my own, and am not surprised to find several references to the Rainbow Bridge. Before my first visit to the Dog Chapel many years ago, I'd never heard of or seen a reference to the Rainbow Bridge. But as I walked through the sanctuary reading the heartfelt letters and notes for the first time, I saw that it was mentioned over and over again by those who'd lost their pets and believed they'd be reunited with them in the afterlife.

I created a picture of it in my mind back then—a beautiful wooden bridge that curved over a clear, dark blue stream, on the other side of which, arching above the distant green hills, was a rainbow. The bridge was the passageway from this life to the next, a calming and comforting image.

And then, about a year ago, shortly after Laika died, I received a sympathy card that provided me with a much more detailed vision of the Rainbow Bridge than the one I'd created for myself. The card was from the staff at Angel View Pet Cemetery, where Laika had been cremated. When her ashes were returned to us we found the card tucked in alongside her urn. Printed inside the card was the following, credited to Author Unknown:

> *Rainbow Bridge*
>   *Just this side of Heaven is a place called Rainbow Bridge. When an animal dies that has been especially close to someone here, that pet goes to Rainbow Bridge. There are meadows and hills for all of our special friends so they can run and play together. There is plenty of food, water and sunshine, and our friends are warm and comfortable.*
>   *All the animals who had been ill and old are restored to health and vigor. Those who were hurt or*

maimed are made whole and strong again, just as we
remember them in our dreams of days and times gone
by. The animals are happy and content, except for one
small thing; they each miss someone very special to them,
who had to be left behind.

They all run and play together, but the day comes
when one suddenly stops and looks into the distance. His
bright eyes are intent. His eager body quivers. Suddenly
he begins to run from the group, flying over the green
grass, his legs carrying him faster and faster.

You have been spotted, and when you and your
special friend finally meet, you cling together in joyous
reunion, never to be parted again. The happy kisses rain
upon your face; your hands again caress the beloved
head, and you look once more into the eyes of your
trusting pet, so long gone from your life but never absent
from your heart.

Then you cross the Rainbow Bridge together . . ."

I don't know what happens when we die, not in any way for
which I can offer up concrete proof. But the afterlife isn't about
proof—it's about belief and faith. I believe in the existence of
the Rainbow Bridge, have faith that one day I'll cross it and be
reunited for eternity with every being I've ever loved and lost.
And I'm not alone in my belief. The walls of the Dog Chapel
are filled with the words of others who believe.

"To Baylin and Champ . . . We miss you, love you, and will
meet you at Rainbow Bridge."

"Molly—I miss you more every day—we will be reunited
again at the rainbow bridge."

"Bless all those I helped cross the bridge."

"To my sweet Dixieland Delight, May you run happy and
painfree across the Rainbow Bridge. Though we only had each
other for a short time, I loved you more than you will ever know."

While browsing in a bookstore not long ago, I purchased
a small, recently published book by Friar Jack Wintz entitled

I Will See You in Heaven. Friar Jack views the question of whether or not we'll see the animals we love again as not only an essential one, but as a broader inquiry on whether God intends all of creation to experience salvation, or just human-kind. Using examples from the Bible, Friar Jack sets out to explore this question.

He wonders, for example, why God would pronounce all creatures "very good" in Genesis 1:31 but exclude them from heaven. He questions why God would have commanded Noah to bring two of every animal species with him on the ark to be saved from the flood if animals weren't also a part of God's ultimate plan. And finally, he points to Revelations 5:13, in which John recounts a vision he's had of heaven: God is sitting on a throne and Jesus, who has taken on the form of a lamb, stands nearby. John says: "Then I heard every creature in heaven and on earth and in the sea, everything in the universe cry out: 'To the one who sits on the throne and to the Lamb be blessing and honor, glory and might, forever and ever.'"

And so the question becomes not so much "Will I see my animals in heaven?" but "Why wouldn't I see my animals in heaven?" This is the question on which faith can be built—the kind of faith that brings those whose dogs are sick or injured or dying to the Dog Chapel to pray, the kind of faith that enables us to believe we'll see our beloved dogs again, and ultimately, the kind of faith that enables us to let them go.

The Word of Dog
FAITH

"Dear Blessed Mother—Please watch over the soul of my Sparky and the life of my Oreo!"

"My dearest Peter, you were my best friend growing up. I think about all our memories when I showed you at the fair, when you fetched apples in the orchard, when you followed me where ever I went. When I went away for college you would wait on the steps knowing when I would be home. You are one of the greatest loves of my life. You have taught me so many important lessons, and I think about you every day. You will always be alive in my heart. I know God has given you wings and has made a special place for you. We will be together again someday. Until then I know you are watching over me. You will remain in my heart forever."

"Nugget—Faithful and true to the last beat of his heart."

"Luca, Candy, Fawn, Ynnue, Apache, Kaj, Neige, Jack—All the dogs that have blessed my life with the unconditional love that is natural to dogs. May God shower you with the blessings with which you bless mankind."

"To my Astor, I think about you all the time and miss you terribly. I will always remember the wonderful times we had together and how much happiness you brought me. Your spirit resides in my heart forever. Someday, I pray, we will meet again and never part company. I love you!"

"Dear Chloe, You are greatly missed by all of us. Our lives are not the same without you. However, we know that we will see you again one day in Heaven. God created you so we know that you are there with Him. May everyone know that God loves us all!!"

"Hoagie—We loved our black lab! So faithful to his family. We will never forget him."

"We love and miss you very much Sammy and could never replace the devoted love and faithfulness you gave us. We also learned so much from your 13 fabulous years on earth."

"Monty and Bucky—May you two find each other in doggy heaven and feel my love! I miss you both."

"Abigail Jeanne: God's Angel Now. For God is love. All things that come from Him return to Him. 'No eye has seen, no ear has heard, no heart can conceive what God has prepared for you.' 1st Corinthians 2:9. 'And he that sat upon the throne said, Behold, I make all things new. And he said unto me, Write: for these words are true and faithful.' Revelation 21:5. The next time it will be forever, a forever with no end."

TWENTY-TWO

THE WORD "PEACE" is not the first word that comes to mind when I reflect on the last five months of Chispa's life. In fact, that word doesn't enter my mind at all. There was little if any peace, for her or for me and Marisel. But it's different now—she's gone, led out of this life wrapped in our arms and our fierce love for her, and I'm sure she's in a place of even greater love, finally at peace. And with time, when grief has run its course, there will be peace for me as well.

I walk over to the stained glass window bearing the word "Peace" and stand before it. The image on this window is of a black Lab with a golden halo floating over her head—an angel dog, now with God. Is this what it takes, I wonder, to find true peace—a permanent date with the Almighty? Is it possible to experience an enduring sense of peace while alive? I stare at the image on the window, as if expecting the word "Peace" to transform itself into another word, perhaps even an entire sentence, that will provide the answer to this question. But the five letters stare back at me unchanged, challenging me to find my own answer.

Peace is both defined and experienced as a sense of quiet, calm, and tranquility, a certain type of stillness in the mind and heart. But at its core, I find it closely related to and perhaps even dependent upon freedom—freedom from wanting, from grasping, from holding on to love and life too tightly, either refusing or not knowing how to let go. All who've become congregants of the Dog Chapel have learned to let go, and the notes left behind are testament both to the pain and hope that accompany surrendering a beloved dog to new life. But buried beneath the words posted on the chapel walls, beneath the layers of tumultuous emotions those words represent, is a deep and abiding sense of peace. And perhaps it's this that draws me over and over again to this most unusual place of worship, this that forms and sustains my faith.

I want to write one last note before leaving. I select a light blue post-it, and with fine-point blue ink begin to put my words to paper.

> "To our sweet girl Chispa: We heard the bell, and know you are free. Thank you, angel dog—for the bell, and for everything else. We'll see you again. Your Moms."

I pin the note on the rear wall of the sanctuary, directly beneath the remembrance I wrote a short time ago for her and Laika. Lingering in the Dog Chapel for just one more moment, I look around, take it all in—love and loss and gratitude and grief all weaving their way through and around each other, testaments to thousands of journeys that have ended in the ultimate peace, the peace that passes all understanding. I say one last prayer for the souls remembered on the countless pieces of overlapping paper that surround me, then walk out of the Dog Chapel and into the sunlight.

The Word of Dog
PEACE

"Stella—What a beautiful, majestic dog! You took such good care of everyone, people and animals alike. We miss your singing and your hugs. We loved you as much as you loved us. Be at peace."

"Paddy, It still hurts, but you do not, and that is all that matters. You were the best dog ever."

"Maxie. I got adopted from a shelter and had a very good life. I loved my yard, my park, and my people. I am at peace."

"Odin, you are so loved and will never be forgotten. You live forever in your momma's heart. You don't have to worry because Koda has come to take care of your boy and bring laughter back into your home. Run and dig free at the bridge, sweet puppy!"

"O.J., not for orange juice—I remember you as a puppy. I remember you as a dog. I remember you always. We will miss you dearly, baby O.J. You taught me to love and be gentle. Have your peace now."

"Hogan, When you were a pup I promised that I would be with you until 'the end.' How fortunate we were to have each other. Being with you on 'Bella Luna' and sharing the ride was a true gift. All of your friends at work miss you and talk about

you every day. Uncle Larry has thanked me for
sharing your last days with him. Rest now, peace
my friend . . . and I will see you at Rainbow
Bridge."

"To my buddy Mato—The years have passed since
I wandered through the wilds with you but I think
about you every day. My dreams are filled with
your youth & you run up to me and wag your tail
& give me the look that you are happy in the next
world."

"Violet—I layed you down outside the Dog Chapel.
I carried you around for over a year and can't think
of a better place for you."

"A note to our beloved Kysha to say "Thank you"
for sharing your life with us. We feel very fortunate
to have enjoyed your friendship and companionship
for fourteen wonderful years. You gave so much,
and asked so little in return. Your memories will live
on forever in a very special place deep within our
hearts. We miss you more than words can express,
yet we are comforted to know that you are at
peace. This is not goodbye forever, Just so long for
now."

Gail Gilmore is a career advisor at Harvard University's Faculty of Arts and Sciences, and a volunteer for Missing Dogs Massachusetts. She lives in the Boston area with her spouse and two Puerto Rican rescue dogs. *Dog Church* is her first book.